The Persian Room Presents

The Persian Room

An Oral History
of New York's
Most Magical
Night Spot

Room

Presents

P A T T Y   F A R M E R

VANTAGEPress
New York

Copyright © 2012 by Patty Farmer

Published by Vantage Press, Inc.
419 Park Ave. South, New York, NY 10016

Manufactured in the United States of America

ISBN 978-0-533-16511-7
Library of Congress Catalog Card No 2011913365

0   9   8   7   6   5   4   3   2

Cover and interior design by Victor Mingovits
Cover and interior illustrations by Sujean Rim
Photo credits appear on page 223

Vantage Press and the Vantage Press colophon
are registered trademarks of Vantage Press, Inc.

ACKNOWLEDGMENTS

It's with much gratitude and admiration that I thank and applaud the brilliant cadre of luminaries who so graciously shared with me their memories, impressions, and memorabilia related to gracing the Persian Room stage. I am especially grateful to those who told the stories of others who are no longer here to share their own recollections. As enchanting as the Persian Room was—and it was—it was still just a room. Its especially bewitching sparkle and luster emanated from the extraordinary parade of musicians, magicians, dance teams, comedians, singers, and other entertainers who passed through it with such style during the five decades when it was a New York City fixture.

I'd especially like to express my deep affection and gratitude to Hilary Knight for his extraordinary assistance in providing background, suggestions, research, and inspiration.

I would also like to thank the smart, creative, and dedicated professionals who helped bring this book to life in such style: David Lamb, Laura Ross, and Selina Peyser at Vantage Press; Sujean Rim for her delightful illustrations; and Victor Mingovits for his stylish design.

Without the cooperation of the good people at Photofest, D'Arlene Studios, Bettmann/Corbis, the Museum of the City of New York Manuscripts and Ephemera Collection, and Sony Music Entertainment, this would be a less lively book, indeed. And I'd like to extend a special thank-you to the artists who provided me with photographs and artifacts from their personal collections.

For every star
that shone so brightly
on the Persian Room stage

CONTENTS

INTRODUCTION

The entrance to the Persian Room after its

lavish 1950 transformation.

In 1955, after a successful career

in entertainment, the legendary

Kay Thompson dreamed up

and introduced to the world a

precocious six-year-old girl named

Eloise, who lived at the elegant

Plaza Hotel in New York City

with her nanny and a few rather

eccentric pets. With no parents in

sight, Eloise concocted her own

adventures and, throughout the

course of six books, won the hearts of millions of children and adults worldwide, introducing them to the delights of the magical Plaza Hotel in the process. (Her picture still hangs prominently in the lobby, and to this day, many make a pilgrimage just to see the place this fictional force of nature turned upside down on a daily basis!)

Growing up, I was among those little girls who read about Eloise and dreamed of life at the Plaza—and guess what? Sometimes dreams *do* come true! Nowadays I am lucky enough to live in a condominium at the Plaza with my own singular menagerie: two fastidious and bossy tea-cup-size French poodles named Sabrina and Marina.

I may not have managed to score Eloise's penthouse, but I live in a lovely spot on the eighth floor overlooking Central Park. Snuggled on my window seat I can see the gaily hued canopy of the carousel in the summer and the bundled-up, red-faced skaters frolicking at Wollman Rink in the winter. Year round I hear the clop, clop, clop of the horse-drawn carriages that have been ferrying people around the neighborhood since the turn of the nineteenth century.

I love roaming around the recently rejuvenated building, most of which is still a bustling hotel and favorite New York City attraction. There's the breathtaking beauty of the stained-glass dome ceiling over the Palm Court, unveiled for the first time since the 1950s, when Conrad Hilton had the ceiling dropped to accommodate newfangled central air conditioning—the height of modern luxury at the time. The Oak Bar and Oak Room have been scrubbed, buffed,

FRED STERRY
President

OHN D. OWEN
Manager

DISTINGUISHED by its world-famous reputation; ideally lo-
ated on Fifth Avenue, facing the attractive vista of Central Park.

OFFERING its guests the unique privilege of quiet atmos-
here with accessibility to fashionable shops and theatres.

•

Fifty-ninth Street and Fifth Avenue.

The PLAZA New York

A 1946 advertisement for the Plaza Hotel.

and polished until they sparkle. Even the braid on the door-men's fancy coats seems to have new luster. And here's the best part: like Eloise, I can summon room service whenever I want—though I tend to order more than the six raisins she favored.

Life at the Plaza is the best—but there's one beautiful part of it that exists only in memory: the Persian Room.

Today, if you visit the Champagne Bar and Rose Room, you are standing where the Persian Room used to be—and what a unique and marvelous place it was! For some reason, Kay Thompson rarely allowed Eloise to sneak into the Persian Room—although she herself performed there many times. But I can imagine the spunky six-year-old spying on its elegant patrons and performers from under-neath its tablecloths or behind its fancy draperies.

For more than forty years, from 1934 to 1975, the Persian Room was the place to be. An unparalleled array of performers graced its stage—anyone who was anyone in entertainment was thrilled to accept an engagement. And, though more than three decades have passed since the final ovation, there are many who remember this extrav-agant nightclub. Because I dearly love my home and its history, I want to take you on a magical, delightful journey back to those halcyon days of refinement and sophistica-tion. Come along as we step into a time when ladies and gentlemen were chic and debonair, when everyone was coiffed and made up and ready for the time of their lives. At the Persian Room, the couple at the next table might be Elizabeth Taylor and Richard Burton, Frank Sinatra and Ava Gardner, Katharine Hepburn and Spencer Tracy, or John F. Kennedy and Jackie. Or perhaps you'd spot the celebrated chanteuse Hildegarde on a night away from performing there herself.

I can't wait to introduce you to the people who knew firsthand what it was like to entertain and be entertained in the Persian Room. I talked to as many of them as I could find, and they were extremely happy to share their stories.

What are we waiting for? Let's begin our journey at the beginning.

CHAPTER ONE

The 1930s

Lillian Gaertner Palmedo puts the finishing touches on one of her murals, specially commissioned by designer Joseph Urban, in anticipation of the Persian Room's 1934 opening.

In 1934, the country was emerging from the Depression. Prohibition had finally been repealed, and Henry Rost, the operating manager of the Plaza, seized the opportunity to shake things up a little at the landmark hotel. He decided to create a stylish room where fashionable people could meet for cocktails, dinner, and dancing. He believed that if he could get the details just right, it would become a "hot spot"—a destination for celebrities and socialites as well as the cherished guests of the hotel.

To realize his vision, Rost knew he needed more than a conventional architect or interior designer. He hired Ziegfeld Follies scene designer Joseph Urban to transform the former Rose Room into something truly special: a kind of nightly sojourn to exotic Persia. With characteristic flair, Urban adorned the walls with five exquisite murals by Lillian Palmedo, depicting luxuriant scenes of hunting, dancing, singing, eating, and drinking, Persian-style. Red dominated the color scheme, from the crimson velvet drapes and plush ruby-colored chairs to the burgundy-dappled carpets, and all was splashed with vivid blue accents. As his crowning touch, Urban installed a massive twenty-seven-foot bar to celebrate the demise of Prohibition.

On April 1, 1934, the Persian Room officially opened with an afternoon benefit for the New York Infirmary for Women and Children. That evening the Renee and Tony De Marco dance team, accompanied by the Emil Coleman Orchestra, entertained the swank crowd into the early hours of the morning. In the audience was an assortment of personalities: socialites, captains of industry, royalty, and New York debutantes with their beaus. Small linen-draped tables were set with china, crystal, and gleaming mono-grammed silver flatware. Huge bouquets scented the room, and the chandeliers, festooned with thousands of dangling

Eddy Duchin tickles the Persian Room ivories,

as John Roosevelt and Sally Clark join the fun.

DAISIES

Gin .... .55
    Gin, Grenadine, Lemon Juice, Fruit
Sloe Gin .... .65
    Sloe Gin, Grenadine, Lemon Juice, Fruit
Brandy .... .90
    Brandy, Grenadine, Lemon Juice, Fruit
Rum .... .65
    Jamaica Rum, Grenadine, Lemon Juice, Fruit

JULEPS

Mint .... .85
    Bourbon Whiskey, Sugar, Brandy Top, Fresh
    Mint
Brandy 1.10
    Brandy, Sugar, Rum Top, Fresh Mint
Major Bailey .... .85
    Gin, Sugar, Fresh Mint, Lemon Juice

LONG DRINKS

Amer Picon .... .70
    Amer Picon, Grenadine or Curaçao,
    Carbonic
Black Velvet 1.70
    Split of Guinness's Sto
    Champagne
Gin Buck ....
    Gin, Lemon Juice, Split
Horse's Neck ......
    Imp. Ginger Ale, Who
Mamie Taylor .....
    Scotch, Lime and Lim
    Peel, Ginger Ale
Pernod à l'Eau (Ab
    Pernod, Lump of Su
Rum Collins .....
    Rum, Lemon Juice,
Tom Collins....
    Gin, Lemon Juice,
Brandy Collins ..
    Brandy, Lemon Ju

Drink List

The
Persian Room
at the Plaza

A Persian Room drink menu from 1936.

teardrop crystals, sent sparkles everywhere. The price of this night on the town? Three dollars for dinner and the show, or $1.50 for supper only. But really, who would want to eat and run? Newspapers praised the opening as "the best night club soirée since Prohibition ended."

For the remainder of the 1930s and well into the '40s, exhibition dancing and big band orchestras were the main attractions at the Persian Room and other fashionable nightclubs.

The De Marco dance team featured Tony along with a series of partners—his successive wives—throughout the 1930s and '40s. Nina was followed by Renée and then Sally. It was Renée who appeared with Tony at the Persian Room that historic opening night, and on several other occasions until 1940. Interestingly, all three teams were reviewed as among the most successful exhibition ballroom dancers.

Veloz and Yolanda were another pair of nationally acclaimed ballroom dancers that graced the Persian Room stage. Yolanda Casazza was born in New York's "Little Italy" in 1908. She met Frank Veloz at a roadside speakeasy in 1920, and though it wasn't an instant love match, they liked to dance together and soon had racked up more than forty trophies from dance contests. They married and were known for their fabulous costumes—designed by Frank—and their improvisational style. Their exhibitions at the Persian Room were great fun because they were virtually unrehearsed and different each time.

Between rounds of the club circuit, Veloz and Yolanda opened dance studios in Southern California and danced in such films as *Champagne Waltz* (1937), *Pride of the Yankees* (1942), and *Cavalcade of Dance* (1943), for which they earned an Oscar nomination.

Leo Reisman led the most sought-after "society" orchestra of the period. Born in 1897, he began studing the violin at age ten, and by the time he was a young teenager, he was playing in hotel bands. At twenty-two, he established his own band and performed at many of New York's best venues, including the Persian Room. He recorded over eighty hits, including *Stormy Weather* (1933) and *You Kiss While You're Dancing* (1934).

Eddy Duchin was born in Cambridge, Massachusetts, in 1909. Discovering his natural talent for the piano at a young age, he joined the Leo Reisman Orchestra in 1929. Thanks to his good looks as much as his talent, he soon became one of the country's most sought-after young bandleaders, repeatedly billed as "the Adonis of the supper club maestros." Needless to say, he was a hit with Persian Room audiences.

Sadly, Eddy died young, at the age of forty-one, from leukemia. But he packed a lot of living into the years he had. By 1934 he had developed a national following for his performances on radio shows and in 1936 was featured on *The Burns and Allen Show*. During that same time frame he was in a few movies—*Coronado* (1935) and *Hit Parade of 1937*—all while appearing at the Persian Room.

Eddy's son, Peter, continued in his fathers footsteps, taking up the baton with the Peter Duchin Orchestra. And yes, he also made a splash at the Persian Room, playing there for New Year's Eve in 1973 and 1974.

Some other wonderful Persian Room performers from the 1930s:

· Eve Becke
· The Ray Benson Orchestra
· The Emil Coleman Orchestra
· Dario and Diane
· Paul Draper
· The Hartmans
· The Henry King Orchestra
· Lydia and Jareaco
· Mario and Florio
· Maurine and Norva
· Pancho's Orchestra
· Jane Pickens
· Ramon and Rosita
· George Sterney
· Eve Symington

CHAPTER TWO

The 1940s

The dance team of Sally and Tony De Marco.

Tony and another wife, Renée, were the first performers

at the Persian Room, on April 1, 1934.

It was in the '40s that American women entered the workplace in a major way, filling thousands of jobs vacated by men going off to war. Rosie the Riveter became a symbol of patriotism and can-do spirit for a new generation of empowered women. When, to everyone's joy, the war ended, those women went back to their homes and families—but they weren't the same. They'd had a taste of independence, and there would be no going back—not completely.

Radio was the main source of entertainment as well as information, bringing music, soap operas, game shows, and comedies, as well as news and sports, into living rooms across the country. Television had been introduced at the 1939 World's Fair, but it wasn't available to consumers until 1947. Even then, programming was extremely limited, and only a few privileged families owned one.

Fashions were austere in the early '40s because the War Production Board set strict limits on the amount of fabric allowed in the construction of garments. American designers compensated for cloth rationing by creating a new style of women's suits: short skirts topped by petite jackets. Nylon stockings were outlawed, forcing fashion-conscious ladies to draw simulated stocking seams down the backs of their legs with eyebrow pencils. New York designers, cut off from Paris couture, began to create new, peculiarly American garments—leisure outfits and less-constructed fashions that emphasized comfort and suited a more active, less formal lifestyle. Soon, the United States was the sportswear capital of the world.

In music, it was the era of the big bands and the exuberant dance known as the jitterbug. The most popular singers, including Bing Crosby, Dinah Shore, Perry Como, and Frank Sinatra, sang with the big bands before embarking on solo careers. John Birks "Dizzy" Gillespie introduced the generation to the sinewy, rebellious sounds of bebop and modern jazz. In baseball, Jackie Robinson led the Brooklyn Dodgers to six World Series.

Frozen dinners, computers, the bra, Tupperware, Dr. Spock, microwave ovens, the atom bomb, Slinkies, the Zoot Suit, aluminum foil, radar, penicillin, and pin-up girls all came to prominence in the 1940s. Humphrey Bogart, Jimmy Stewart, Joan Crawford, Betty Davis, Cary Grant, Doris Day, and hundreds of other stars were idolized for their larger-than-life glamour and for the ageless films they brought to life. As a repercussion of World War II, many fine European artists immigrated to the United States, and the nucleus of the art world moved from Paris to New York.

It won't surprise you to learn, however, that life in the Persian Room of the '40s held itself aloof from the harsher realities of the decade. Not unlike the escapist fare gracing movie screens about town, it provided those fortunate enough to afford a table an elegant refuge from the events of the day, though, when it came to raising money for war bonds, the Persian Room certainly did its part. And it offered a respite to the performers, too, many of whom had spent time overseas entertaining the troops and boosting morale.

.　　.　　.　　.　　.

WHO BETTER TO start with, when evoking New York's finest night spot in the '40s, than Marge Champion? A living legend now in her nineties, she and her husband Gower were regulars at the Persian Room throughout the decade, with a devoted following. She was all too happy to reminisce—and her memory for the glorious details couldn't have been sharper.

The first thought that popped into my head upon meeting Marge in the New York apartment that she's occupied for thirty-seven years was that the research from Quin, one of my trusty assistants, was faulty. No way this beautiful woman was ninety-two. But she is. I was invited to her home the day after she returned from Los Angeles, where she participated in something called *Christmas with Walt Disney* at the Walt Disney Family Museum. She actually pulled a muscle doing one of her high kicks there, recreating one of the routines she'd performed as a model for *Snow White* many decades earlier. Yes, high kicks!

"It seems as if you're out and about an awful lot, going to dance exhibits and all the Disney events," I commented. "Are you ever going to slow down?"

"You're right. I thought I'd be able to finally read some of the books on my shelves that I've never gotten to, but I'm so busy with all the appearances and requests I get but it's a definite blessing. I still take classes downstairs in the

Marge Champion in her prime. Now in her 90s,
she is still doing those high kicks!

gym. There are a couple of gals who teach them that are wonderful, and I enjoy it because it sure keeps me going."

Marge was dancing almost as soon as she could walk, thanks to her father, Ernest Belcher. Ernest was the first dance director for motion pictures, and Marge told me that he'd worked with most of the top movie stars of the day, including Charlie Chaplin, Mary Pickford, Mack Sennett, Fred Astaire, Mae Murrey, Shirley Temple, and John Gilbert.

By the time Marge was twelve, she was her father's assistant and demonstrator. "He'd call me in and ask me to show Tula Ellice Finklea [later known as Cyd Charisse] how a certain step or dance was done," she told me.

In the late 1930s and early '40s, Marge worked for Disney Studios as the moving model for Snow White, *Pinocchio's* Blue Fairy, Hyacinth Hippo in *Fantastia*, and numerous other characters that decades of children still love today. Though she played small roles in such films as *Honor of the West, Sorority House*, and *The Story of Vernon and Irene Castle*, stage work was her bread and butter. She appeared in *Portrait of a Lady, Beggar's Holiday, The Little Dog Laughed*, and many other plays over her long career.

I have to interrupt Marge's story for a minute to tell you about her husband and dancing partner of thirty years, Gower Champion. Gower was only fourteen when he and his friend Jeanne Tyler entered and won the Veloz and Yolanda Waltz to Fame dance contest. A week's booking at the Coconut Grove was the prize. With his mother, Beatrice,

— *35* —

along to chaperone and help oversee negotiations, Gower and Jeanne, billed as "America's Youngest Dance Team," hit the road. They were successful not only in top-drawer New York nightclubs, but Gower also found work in featured dance roles in Broadway musicals such as *Streets of Paris* and *Count Me In.*

America's Youngest Dance Team broke up when Gower joined the Coast Guard during World War II.

"When Gower got out of the service he never wanted to be part of a dance team again," Marge told me. "He got a studio on the East Side of New York in an old church, with a huge room where he could choreograph and do things like that. Well, unfortunately, things didn't go exactly as he planned, and he had to become part of a team again."

When he tried to recruit Jeanne and resurrect their old act, he found her married and uninterested in picking up where America's Youngest Dance Team had left off. So in 1945 he went to Ernest Belcher, his former dance instructor, for advice. Ernest said, "Ask my daughter Marge; maybe she'd be interested." Clearly her interest went further than just dancing, and the feeling was mutual. They married on October 5, 1947.

"Right after Gower and I got married, we flew East and did a show with Milton Berle for television, which, in those days, practically no one saw because there just weren't that many TV sets. At the end of that week, we opened for Liberace at the Persian Room.

"For some strange reason—because Lee rarely got a bad review—we got better notices than he did. So Mame Abbott, who booked our engagement there, booked us again a year later, on our first wedding anniversary. This time we topped the bill, and that was very satisfying."

In their Persian Room engagements, Marge and Gower Champion didn't just perform for politely seated spectators; they led the diners in the latest in ballroom and swing dancing with their own unique twist, making even the tango, waltz, and mambo look easy. "My father trained me as a ballet dancer, and Gower taught me the other styles, and new dances and steps were always being introduced," Marge explained.

"We were certainly never just a dance team. Our act was more like a musical revue—mostly dancing. We sang and talked and joked, all things that dance teams didn't generally do.

"There wasn't another room like the Persian Room, and because it was such an intimate space, it was friendly to us. We could talk to each other or directly to someone in the audience. Supper club audiences differ from stage audiences. You perform *for* stage audiences, but in supper clubs like the Persian Room, you have to make real contact with your audience or you don't get far.

"My father taught me there was a reason behind every movement. At the end of a number you don't just put out your hands. You have to think, 'There you are.' I think that's why we captured people. Gower never extended his hand to me just to swing me around. He always *gave me his hand*. There's a difference. David Craig, Nancy Walker's husband, used to teach that. Subtext.

"We came back on our sixth anniversary in 1953. By that time we had the Cheerleaders with us. They sang an opening number and introduced us through the lyrics of the song. They also occupied audiences while we made quick wardrobe changes. They'd sing, and I'd change in the kitchen.

"One of the big treats of performing there was that you got to stay at the Plaza for the run of your show—though they put us up in what used to be the maids' quarters, on the top floors. Going up to the room to change was out of the question, of course."

When the Plaza converted some of the units to condominiums in 2007, those maids' quarters were sold as penthouses and commanded prices starting at twenty million dollars!

During the 1950s, the Champions made Hollywood their home and turned most of their energy to film work. They appeared in Paramount's *Mr. Music* with Bing Crosby, the 1951 MGM revival of the musical *Show Boat*, *Everything I Have is Yours* (1952), and *Give a Girl a Break* (1953). In 1957 *The Marge and Gower Champion Show* on CBS shadowed their own story as they played two dancers trying to get out of show business.

They found fame on Broadway in the 1960s, choreographing and winning awards for such hits as *Bye, Bye*

Birdie in 1961, *Hello Dolly* in 1964, and *I Do! I Do*! in 1966. The Champions divorced in 1973, and Gower continued his successful career on Broadway, passing away just hours before winning a Tony for *42nd Street*. At ninety-two, Marge is still amazing, sharp as a razor, traveling, giving lectures and talks, and occasionally performing. She may have lasted a few decades longer than the Persian Room itself, but she certainly cherishes her memories of the place. I'm just trying to persuade her to be a little more sparing with her high kicks!

.   .   .   .   .

AS I MENTIONED, though they remained a bastion of elegance, the Plaza and Persian Room did their part in the war effort by raising literally millions in war bond sales. "The bigger the bond, the better the view" was the mantra for war bond fashion shows and auctions. And what was the reward for buying a hefty $1,000 bond? Ringside seats at a Persian Room performance by "the incomparable Hildegarde," by far the most beloved chanteuse of her day. At one show, a Hildegarde rendition of "The Last Time I Saw Paris" inspired a well-heeled fan to swell the coffers of the war effort to the tune of $25,000.

With her first performance there, at a Soldiers' and Sailors' Club benefit on September 23, 1941, Hildegarde (born Hildegarde Loretta Sell in Adell, Wisconsin, in 1906) changed the Persian Room forever. Eleanor Roosevelt called her "the first lady of supper clubs" (and she would know), and Hildegarde was described waggishly by gossip columnist Walter Winchell as "the dear that made Milwaukee famous." No stranger to fame himself, Liberace described Hildegarde as "perhaps the most famous supper club entertainer who ever lived," while no less a personage than King Gustavus V of Sweden dubbed her "the girl with the eternal touch of Spring." But to all who loved her, she will always be known by the indelible moniker ascribed to Winchell: the Incomparable Hildegarde!

Hildegarde was a sultry, sophisticated singer, regal yet somehow approachable and funny. She was renowned for wearing chic over-the-elbow gloves, even when playing the piano, a signature that resulted from the time an orchestra leader inadvertently skipped her lead-in and she had no time to remove them. In an instant, she discovered she was comfortable playing with them on, and the rest was history. She wielded lace handkerchiefs flirtatiously and bestowed roses on her audience at the close of each show.

Sadly, I never had an opportunity to meet Hildegarde—she passed away quietly in a New York City hospital at the age of ninety-nine in 2005. But over a luscious steak dinner in the Plaza's Oak Room, Don Dellair, Hildegarde's last manager, reminisced and told me story after story about her.

"It was Hildegarde who made the Persian Room, and

the Persian Room that made Hildegarde," he said. "I wasn't Hildegarde's manager when she began, I was just a teen-ager. Her manager then was Anna Sosenko, and Anna was something else. It all began when Hildy was performing across the street, at the Savoy Plaza. Anna came here to speak to the people at the Plaza about her. She said, 'She sings, she plays piano, she is witty, funny, and glamorous. She wears gorgeous stuff, and you should try her here at the Persian Room!' And that was how it all started.

"When Hildy played here, she did more weeks than anyone else. Everyone else got four weeks; Hildy got six months. Her favorite color was pink, and before they opened for a new season, the entire Persian Room was painted pink for Hildegarde. She literally put the Persian Room on the map: people started writing about it and saying things about it, like, 'They've painted the room.... Hildegarde must be coming!'

"Prior to her, they didn't really have headliners; they had a lot of great orchestras and wonderful dance teams, but Hildegarde was the first headliner. The Persian Room became famous because of Hildy's appearances there—but at the same time, Hildy became a household name because of the Persian Room.

"I want to talk about Anna for a moment," Don said as he pushed his very clean plate away, leaned back, and stretched a bit, "because she was very much a part of this story, too. Anna was a great manager but very controlling.

An ad for the Incomparable
Hildegarde, who was called
"the first lady of supper
clubs" by no less an expert
than Eleanor Roosevelt.

You want someone like that working for you. Anna insisted on working the lighting for Hildy's shows, and she once turned them out in the middle of Hildy's performance. I wasn't there, but I've heard the story many times. Apparently, Hildy didn't do something Anna had told her to do, so Anna just blacked out the lights and walked away!

"Always the trouper, Hildy didn't miss a beat. 'Oh, Alex,' she called, 'Alextrician!' That got a big laugh from the audience, who naturally thought it was part of the act, so she started using it all the time. Anna eventually came back and turned the lights back on. She was brilliant, but you had to do what she said. Hildegarde didn't mind a bit because she was a performer and just wanted to perform. She didn't want to worry or even think about the business side of things."

Although the Persian Room was her artistic home, Hildegarde performed in other clubs and on celebrated stages around the world. In addition to entertaining the likes of King Gustavus V of Sweden, King George V, and

King George VI, she performed at the White House during both the Truman and Eisenhower presidencies.

Hildegarde's signature songs, "Darling, Je Vous Aime Beaucoup" and "The Last Time I Saw Paris," mesmerized audiences night after night, month after month, year after year. Broadway and Hollywood stars, denizens of high society, politicians, and heads of state attended Hildegarde's performances from 1941 through 1947. Though her regular annual engagements ended at that point, she returned to the Persian Room on and off until 1975. She was the highest paid supper club entertainer during 1944 and 1945, earning $2,000 to $3,000 per four-week engagement—in addition to a percentage of the house—and with constantly sold-out shows, that amounts to quite a salary.

Don mesmerized me with his stories, but it wasn't until dessert that I was able to pull out a personal memory about one of his first visits to the Persian Room when he was a young man.

"I was in college at this point, and two friends and I wanted to impress our girlfriends. So we decided to take them to the Persian Room to see the incomparable Hildegarde.

When we told the girls we were going, they were so excited they became giddy. Little did they know that once we got there we still had to stand in line—and one's place in line didn't matter. We were at the front of the line, but all the important people were ushered in ahead of us.

"Luckily, a very nice lady stood up for us saying it was disgraceful that we had been waiting so long and demanded to speak to the person in charge. This was a very important woman (though I have no idea to this day who she was), and the head honcho came out and told us to come right in. Well, we might have been better off if we hadn't gotten in. Because when the bill came I looked at it and thought, 'Uh oh! I don't think we have enough.' We had no clue how expensive it would be. We should have known, but we just didn't think about it. At that point, the girls went to the ladies' room and told us to come get them when we had it figured out.

"The maître d' came over and asked us how much we had. We told him and gave it all to him, but it wasn't enough. The dinners were ten dollars each, which was a lot for us. Plus, the cover charge was two dollars a person. He asked us what we thought we should do. And we said we'd give him what we had, go home to Brooklyn, talk to our fathers, and come back later in the week with the balance of what we owed him. The man was so caring that he asked us how we were going to get home because we were giving him all our money. We said we'd take the subway, but he gave us enough money to take the girls home in a cab. He acted like a dad to us. But that was the Persian Room.

"Of course we brought back the money, and when we did, we asked to see the maître d'. 'Wow, you actually came back,' he said. 'I had a feeling you would!'"

Now, that's a Persian Room story—because it's elegant. Everything about the Persian Room was like that.

. . . . .

LIBERACE INITIALLY PLAYED the Persian Room in 1940 as an intermission pianist for thirty-five dollars a week. He didn't return as a headliner until seven years later, on October 12, 1947. And, with the characteristic extravagance that set him apart from all other performers, he brought with him a mind-blowing piano custom built by Julius Bluthner and promoted as the world's largest concert grand. Because of an inconvenient strike in progress, the piano was delivered to the Plaza just in time for Liberace's magnificent entrance, which included the lighting of his candelabra, on display at the Plaza for the first time. He never did a performance without it after that.

Liberace was a remarkably accomplished concert pianist and a consummate showman, telling jokes and engaging the audience by asking for requests and improvising. At one point in his show he canvassed for help and brought a female volunteer up to sit next to him at the piano and assist him in a complicated classical arrangement. Her contribution consisted of hitting one single note on cue.

Liberace's great talent and friendly, humorous, exquisitely produced show whipped the audience to a frenzy. His outrageous wardrobe, featuring sequins, furs, and satins galore, was topped off by jewelry that looked too heavy for a mere man to wear. It almost always included a diamond-and-platinum ring shaped like a miniature piano. As for his personal attributes, *Variety* proclaimed, "Liberace looks like a cross between Cary Grant and Robert Alda." That was a compliment, by the way.

In looking for some personal Liberace stories, I turned once again to Don Dellair, as I knew they'd been good friends since Don's days as a member of the Tommy Wonder and Don Dellair dancing and singing team. (He later retired from performing and started the Don Dellair and Tommy Wonder Management Company.) This time, Don was to meet me at my apartment and pay the necessary attention to Sabrina and Marina, and then we'd head out for dinner. While we sat in my living room, I asked him if he really knew *everyone* from a certain era—or if it just seemed that way.

.   .   .   .   .

"WHEN YOU ARE lucky enough to get to a certain age, as I am, you know people," he responded.

"And you knew Liberace," I said, hoping he'd settle into the subject.

"Yes, he was a friend. A dear, dear soul. No matter what trouble he got into, he was the kindest, most gracious, angel of a person. He knew Hildegarde, you know," Don

*It was always a party with Liberace at the keyboard
(even before he adopted his signature candelabra).*

continued. "It was Tommy and I who introduced them. They were from the same city—Milwaukee. We introduced Hildy to Liberace because they were both our dear friends, and we knew they'd hit it off.

"Liberace's full name was Wladziu Liberace, and I don't know if Hildy told him to do it or if he did it because it worked for her, but he quickly dropped his first name and became known—well-known—as Liberace, although all his friends called him Lee.

"Once, during her show at the Persian Room, Hildy introduced him to the audience. They gave him a very welcoming cheer, and Hildy said, 'I'm from Milwaukee; he has to be from Milwaukee. I am known by one name; he uses one name. I play the piano; he plays the piano; in fact, he copied my whole act.'

"Liberace quickly quipped back, 'But I'm sure I have a few more gowns than you have, darling!' The audience howled. It was a thing of love with those two. Hildegarde introduced the song 'I'll be Seeing You,' and eventually Liberace became very well-known for singing that song."

When I visited with Marge Champion she told me that she remembers a time before she and Gower became headliners, and they opened for Lee (as she called him) that he was always painting—many times something for Hildegarde—and had an easel set up in his Plaza suite. He also always requested a room with a long hallway so he could line up his suede shoes of various colors."

Marge smiled remembering those early years, "We were still in our twenties. He was the star of the show and had premature white hair with streaks. He used to send me to the drug store to get this black hair dye because he didn't want to be seen buying it. I sure got funny looks from the sales ladies because here I was this young girl with blond hair buying black hair color!

"He was a swell guy. We were good friends with both him and his brother, who was also his manager."

It probably won't surprise you to learn that Don and I never did make it out to dinner that night. His stories just kept coming, and three hours later we were still sitting on my couch with the kids asleep on our laps. I would gladly forgo dinner any day of the week to listen to more.

.   .   .   .   .

IMMEDIATELY UPON ENTERING Celeste Holm's palatial Central Park West apartment I was awed by her baby grand piano, situated with a commanding view of the park. But I was more impressed by the diminutive golden man perched on top of it—Celeste's Oscar for her Academy Award–winning performance in *Gentlemen's Agreement*. Although I've seen a few of the much-coveted statuettes over the years, this was my first opportunity to hold one, and it was intoxicating.

I was equally as thrilled to meet ninety-four-year-old Celeste, whose dazzling crystal-blue eyes flashed mischievous sparks as she spoke of years past with an absolute clarity that belied her age.

Celeste and her husband, opera singer Frank Basile, had invited me to visit them and talk about her experiences at the Persian Room in the '40s and '50s. But, before we fell headlong into the past, I had to satisfy my curiosity about the present. I asked Celeste, "What have you been up to lately?"

Frank jumped in, telling me proudly, "We were in Indiana just three weeks ago. I was giving a concert with the Indianapolis Opera. Celeste got up and did the last number with me and was brilliant, and the reviews said... 'Frank who? Celeste Holm holds court!'"

"What was the last number?" I asked.

"'Getting to Know You' from *The King and I*. Not a dry eye in the house while she sang it. I introduced her, saying, 'I'd like to welcome to the stage the legendary, the one and only Celeste Holm.' So, she came out on stage, and I started in, 'Celeste, you know, "It's a very ancient saying—"

At this point, Celeste chimed in, finishing the story—and the opening lyric: "As a teacher I've been learning, / you'll forgive me if I boast, / And I've now become an expert on the subject I like most / Getting to know you / getting to know all about you.... "

Celeste was born in New York, though she traveled extensively throughout her childhood (her father was an insurance adjuster for Lloyd's of London) and attended schools in Europe as well as the United States. She was taking me through her background when Frank explained,

The eternally elegant Celeste Holm.

"Celeste grew up with her parents in Chicago, but she never went to the University of Chicago."

"No, I never went to a university at all," she added, "although all of my biographies say I studied drama there. In fact, I was in high school and the principal suggested I take an advanced course in English offered by the University of Chicago, and I did. I think the university probably decided to take credit for me once I'd become successful. I never had any theatrical training at all, until much later."

"Later," Frank said, "was after she had an Oscar and three Academy Award nominations. That was when Elia Kazan suggested the Actor's Studio."

"After high school I came to New York and beat the pavement like everyone else."

In 1936 Celeste began her stage career, appearing as an ingénue in a stock production in Pennsylvania. That was followed by an offer to travel as the understudy for Ophelia in a production of *Hamlet* starring Leslie Howard. In 1938, Celeste made her New York stage debut in a small part in the short-lived comedy *Gloriana*.

In 1939, she landed her first starring role on Broadway in *The Time of Your Life*, co-starring with another theater newbie, Gene Kelly. Other parts followed, but it was in 1943 that Celeste became a star—singing the naughty (for its day) "I Can't Say No" as Ado Annie in *Oklahoma*. She'd been playing the role for just a few months when she took her first bow at the Persian Room.

"Celeste, how did you fit it all in?" I asked. "Your show didn't end until almost 11 p.m., and then you went on at the Plaza?"

"Well, I only had to be in *one* place at any given time, I guess. The curtain would come down, and I'd run over to the Persian Room. Other entertainers went out and ate or socialized after their shows. I sang."

"I know, but just the energy it took."

"In 1943 I was young, you know!"

Frank proudly chimed in, "The midnight show was the hottest ticket in town after hours, and the reviews... they said the Persian Room was *the* place to go."

He continued, "It was only a year after *Oklahoma*, in 1944, that John C. Wilson created *Bloomer Girl* specifically for Celeste, with her name over the title. She was the toast of the town—she was the toast of Broadway!"

It probably sounds as if Frank was right there with Celeste from the beginning of it all, when actually he didn't enter the scene until 1990. But he has been making up for lost time by diligently organizing, chronicling, and archiving even the smallest details of Celeste's career.

" I just want to know my wife, so from the start I listened to her family and their stories, and we talk everyday about everything. As I go through and try to organize all her letters, notices, reviews, and other material—and we have a storage unit full—I'll ask about this and that. Over the years we've both enjoyed it. Celeste relives all the excitement, and I hear all these wonderful stories."

Following that success, Celeste gave in to Hollywood. In 1946, she signed a contract with Twentieth Century-Fox.

In spite of her defection to the West Coast, though, she continued to appear at the Persian Room when she could fit it into her schedule. "I was working and living at the Plaza late in the '40s—maybe 1949—with my young son Dan. He was the male version of Eloise."

I asked what Persian Room memories stand out above all others. She thought a bit, and then the lightbulb went off. "One very exciting incident occurred right around 1943. I actually helped the FBI apprehend some criminals!"

"Oh my God, yes," remembered Frank. "That's a major story. It really should be kept for Celeste's memoirs," he said—before continuing headlong into the tale. "Celeste had been introduced to some people when she was about ten years old in Paris with her parents. Fast-forward sixteen years to 1943 or '44, and she's in a hit musical, and the couple is in New York—passing bad checks around! They are telling people that they are friends of Celeste Holm's, using her name as collateral or a reference."

Celeste picked it up from there: "The FBI approached me and asked if I knew these people, to which I replied, no, not really. They told me what was going on, and I said, well, they've contacted me and it happens that I know where they will be tomorrow night. They'll be at my show at the Persian Room. They had asked me for tickets! Of course the FBI was very excited. We'll be there, the guys said, and if you just point them out to us, we'll arrest them."

Frank's turn: "Celeste carefully chose a certain red dress so that if any blood was spilt, it wouldn't show!"

Was any blood spilled? I had to know.

"No," said Celeste. "The bad guys came in and sat down and I started my show, but the FBI didn't arrive for the longest time. Don't forget, this was the late show. I tried to think what I should do, so I keep ad-libbing and stalling and all kinds of stuff to keep the show going."

Frank jumps in, "Finally, they show up, and Celeste dramatically points them out from the stage. The FBI men arrest them and the next day the papers have headlines saying: Celeste Holm, Finger Woman!!"

Persian Room patrons got a great encore that night.

It might not be as edge-of-your-seat exciting as helping to apprehend criminals, but I did want to know some particulars about Celeste's act.

Did you sing all the great songs from *Oklahoma*?

"Oh no, I couldn't do that. I wasn't allowed to do it. When you are in a current Broadway show they won't let you sing those songs anywhere else. But I had songs written just for me to sing at the Persian Room.

Frank added, "'Eunice from Tunis' was written just for her. In fact, *Life* magazine did a whole spread of Celeste and her photos and faces for 'Eunice.'"

At that point, Frank looked as if he had just remembered something. "Honey," Frank led Celeste, "everyone came to see you at the Persian Room. Do you remember?"

"Oh, of course I remember. I bet you're thinking of the Duke of Windsor and Mrs. Simpson."

"That's right," said Frank. "They got to know Celeste when she was in *Oklahoma*. They would always visit backstage, and they came to see her at the Persian Room all the time, because they lived at the Plaza. In fact, when the Duke was dying, he asked to see Celeste. She went to entertain him in his last week. And John Kennedy knew you when you were in *Oklahoma*, that's way before he was a senator." He turned to me at that point and said, "They dated, you know."

"You and JFK?" I asked her.

"We went on a few dates," she admitted.

When I was going through some of the many books and papers from Celeste's career, I came across a touching letter written to Celeste from a group of servicemen who said that they had seen *Oklahoma* twice and heard her sing "Eunice from Tunis" at the Persian Room. "The soldiers came to see her religiously," Frank told me.

I found another heartwarming letter from a man, now a grandfather, who was coming to New York, and he wanted Celeste to know that he remembered sitting under a tree in 1946, in occupied and later reclaimed France, when a jeep came by, and a young lady took time from her schedule to make him and his two friends feel like they were home. He had made it back, gotten married, and now had grandchildren, and he often brought them to New York and regaled them with the memory of that day.

It was at Twentieth Century-Fox that Celeste made the first nine movies of her career—and what formidable movies they were. She took home the Oscar in 1947 and went on to play numerous touching and comedic roles. A highlight was her turn as a mental patient in *Snake Pit* (1948), the first film to depict the dark side of mental illness.

Celeste was nominated twice more for Best Supporting Actress, for *Come to the Stable* (1949), in which she played a tennis-playing French nun trying to build a children's hospital—seriously—and in *All About Eve* (1950) with Bette Davis. After completing that film, Celeste decided that she missed performing for a live audience and surprised the industry by buying out the remainder of her Fox contract and heading back to Broadway.

In the '50s, Celeste was enticed back to Hollywood, and she had a chance to showcase her lighter side with musical roles in *The Tender Trap* (1955) with Debbie Reynolds and *High Society* (1956) with Grace Kelly and Bing Crosby. Both costarred Frank Sinatra.

During the next four decades, Celeste kept the airlines in business, traveling between Hollywood and Broadway as well as singing at prestigious clubs including the Persian Room. The reviews of her 1958 Persian Room appearance were as impressive as those from 1943.

Celeste and Frank were such wonderful hosts that before I knew it, four hours had flown by. We made plans to get together again, but before I left, the romantic in me had to find out how this great and still affectionate couple had met.

"It was fate. We were introduced but had actually met two years earlier. And I think Celeste thought I was... hmmm, what did you say?"

"I said you were a very beautiful man."

"I think you said the most beautiful man you had ever seen," Frank twinkled, and he continued. "Actually the formal introduction came about because I was in New York and was asked to sing at a big charity gala in New Jersey, and Celeste was one of the guests. Her ride home had to leave early and asked me if I would drive her home. Of course, I said yes, I would be honored. After I did my part of the show, she asked me if I wanted to sit and eat at her table. So I sat down and we talked. It was a wonderful evening. We danced and then talked all the way home, and just as I was approaching Manhattan, she said 'Oh, no—I'm going to my farm,' which was two hours in the other direction!

"I had a girlfriend at the time, a relationship that I was sorting out. But once I did, I spent all my time with Celeste. We hit it off so quickly as best friends that I was afraid to tell her that I was in love with her. It turned out she was feeling the same. She said I probably don't have much time left in the world, but if I can borrow you for three years.... "

I couldn't help exclaiming, "What a love story!"

"That's what she says! And you know, it's been eleven years."

Celeste and Frank were married on Celeste's eighty-fifth birthday, when Frank was forty-seven, making her one of the original cougars! Good for her. Good for them.

*Some other wonderful Persian Room
performers from the 1940s:*

Fred and Elaine Barry

Victor Borge

Carol Bruce

John Buckmaster

Columbus and Carroll

Ben Cutler's Orchestra

Sally and Tony De Marco

Carmen Rivero

Jayne and Adam DiGatano

Morton Downey

Dick Gasparre and His Orchestra

Bob Grant Orchestra

Paul Haakon

Josephine Houston

Laurette and Clyman

Leni Lynn

Maurice and Cordoba

Sara Ann McCabe

Susan Miller

Jacques Peals

Rolly Rolls

Rosario and Antonio

Larry Siry and His Orchestra

Ted Straeter and His Orchestra

Russell Swann

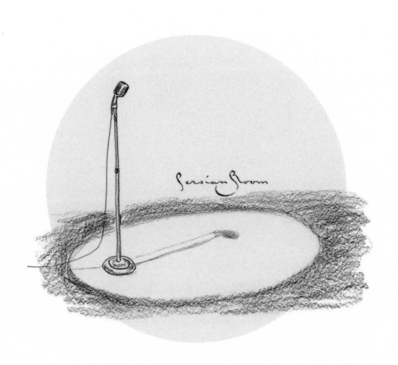

Persian Broom

CHAPTER THREE

The 1950s

A quiet Persian Room prior to opening.

The end of World War II brought thousands of young American men home, and with them came a renewed vitality and passion for fresh beginnings. Returning vets married their sweethearts and began to buy things, including homes outside large cities. *The suburbs* entered the American lexicon, and the baby boom was off to a rousing start.

The decade began as a conservative time: "Under God" was incorporated into the Pledge of Allegiance. Family dynamics and gender roles were precisely defined. Women were housewives; men, providers; and teenagers were expected to mind their elders. (The term *teenager* itself was coined in the '50s.) But there was no holding back social and moral evolution. Under the burgeoning influence of television, movies, radio, and popular magazines, teens developed their own unique style and the rebellious behavior to go with it. It was the period of James Dean jackets and swagger, hula hoops, ducktails, drive-in movies, beehive hairdos, poodle skirts, saddle shoes, and blue jeans. In a more serious vein, the nascent civil rights movement, which gathered steam with the 1954 Supreme Court ruling in *Brown v. Board of Education,* was on its way to becoming a juggernaut, and those formerly complacent housewives began to question their lot and explore their options.

On the music scene, the conservatism of the '40s began to ebb with this new decade. Nightclubs and supper clubs gently phased out exhibition dancing and big band orchestras as the key nightly entertainment, replacing them with headliners from all spheres of show business.

The 1950s gave birth to rock-and-roll. Elvis Presley exploded in popularity, bolstered by controversial appearances on *The Ed Sullivan Show* and *American Bandstand,* TV shows that brought the most up-to-the-moment records

*The sly and comical George Burns and Gracie Allen
were Persian Room favorites in the 1950s.*

and artists into living rooms nationwide. But Ed served up plenty more than rock-and-roll on the *Sullivan Show*, which ran from 1948 to 1971. There was plenty of "grown-up" entertainment, too, and appearances by Liberace, Carol Channing, Sal Mineo, Jane Morgan, Johnnie Ray, Tony Bennett, and many others inspired people to seek out live appearances by these artists in such venues as the Persian Room.

More than ever before, we were presented with diverse musical choices, introduced to different styles and sounds. Bill Haley had us rocking around the clock, while Elvis presented America with his own unique interpretation of rock-and-roll that was so scandalous that when he appeared on TV, the camera could only show him from the waist up. And Chuck Berry...well, Chuck introduced us to a crazy amalgam of blues, rock, and country all wrapped in one crazy package.

On the opposite side of the rock-and-roll coin were the clean-cut heartthrobs, dreamboats, and teen idols. Paul Anka was a "Lonely Boy" who begged us, "Put Your Head on My Shoulder"; Fabian, a "Tiger" begging to be turned loose; and Pat Boone wrote "Love Letters in the Sand" and promised "April Love." Their counterparts were a variety of girl singers that included Patti Page, Patsy Cline, Diahann Carroll, Kay Thompson, and many, many other greats.

We had choices. Country music was a popular pick after Sun Records in Memphis introduced us to the Million Dollar

Quartet: Jerry Lee Lewis, Johnny Cash, Carl Perkins, and—
oh yeah—Elvis.

Music was everywhere. In 1952, Sony's introduction of
the transistor radio made music portable. The hits went
everywhere we did!

In the movies we saw Humphrey Bogart instruct Miss
McCardell to "get reservations at the Persian Room" for
him and Sabrina.

It was an affluent time in New York City: new futuris-
tic museums were inaugurated, Broadway theater thrived,
and contemporary art galleries premiered all over town.
New York became the epicenter of the American cultural
map and has remained so ever since.

So, what was going on at the Plaza? For starters, owner
Conrad Hilton recruited designer Henry Dreyfuss to thor-
oughly revamp the Persian Room. The result was a clean,
modern design in blues and greens. Metallic mesh drapes
custom made by Dorothy Liebes and two striking screens
embellished with a stunning gold-and-white diamond pattern added elegance. And, because no detail was ever
overlooked at the night spot, contemporary china in a coor-
dinating blue-and-green diamond pattern complemented
the scheme. The estimated cost of the transformation was
$200,000, and the revitalized Persian Room reopened with
appropriate fanfare on September 28, 1950.

The swank hotel changed hands in 1955 when Hilton
sold it to the Hotel Corporation of America, controlled by

A. M. Sonnabend. For those of you interested, this was the same year that New York City installed its first three-color traffic signals.

I was fortunate enough to meet some of the best performers to grace the Persian Room stage during the '50s, many of whom are still actively performing. They all agree that there is no modern-day equivalent to the place, especially in its newly decorated 1950s glory.

. . . . .

JULIE WILSON HAS been an American icon and cabaret queen for sixty-five-plus years, celebrated for her dramatically naughty renderings of torch songs, her dazzling designer gowns topped by ostentatious feather boas, and that ubiquitous gardenia behind her left ear.

In 1951, after her show at the posh Mocambo nightclub in Hollywood, Julie met the composer Cole Porter. "Patricia Morrison had told him he should consider putting me in *Kiss Me Kate* because Lisa Kirk was leaving," recounts Julie. "Well, the club manager brought him backstage after the show, and after he introduced us, Mr. Porter looked me up.... and then looked me down.... and didn't say anything for what seemed like a very long time. Then he said 'You'd make a lovely Bianca.' That was that. I got the part, replacing Lisa in the tour heading to London. I stayed on in England for a few years doing *South Pacific* and *Bells Are*

Was there ever a chanteuse more sophisticated
and sultry than Julie Wilson?

Ringing after *Kiss Me Kate.* At the same time, I studied at the Royal Academy of Dramatic Arts.

"At a certain point, I was missing New York, and it was time to start thinking about going home. Luckily, my manager told me he had booked me to open the fall season at the Persian Room."

Arriving home, Julie lived in two worlds: Broadway and supper clubs. After wowing the crowds at the Persian Room, she returned to the theater in *Kismet, Pajama Game,* and others including the 1988 musical *Legs Diamond,* in which she appeared with Peter Allen, singing a song—"The Music Went Out of My Life"—he wrote with her in mind. Although the play was a legendary flop, Julie received a Tony Award nomination.

When Julie and I walked into Manhattan's legendary Russian Tea Room, the lunch patrons might not have immediately recognized her, but there was no mistaking the fact that this svelte, reed-straight, elegant woman was "somebody." Maybe it was her eyes, which still twinkle mischievously, or the come-hither smile that even now turns the heads of men of all ages. I must admit feeling a bit intimidated myself by this meticulously styled and pulled-together, self-assured octogenarian in a fabulous hat.

I say we met for lunch, but show-business people keep their own schedules. "Even though it's 1 p.m., it's breakfast time for me," Julie pointed out. "After so many years of working till the early, early hours and then sleeping until the afternoon, rising late has become a habit."

Looking every bit the gently aging siren, Julie informed the waitress that she needed black coffee, right away.

"Are you still serving breakfast?" she asked.

"No, but how about vichyssoise? Cold soup?"

"My dear," Julie replied, delighted with the opening, "I like my men and my soup *hot!*"

I believe Mae West delivered a version of that line, but Julie's performance was uniquely her own, sweet yet haughty, accompanied by a coy flutter of eyelashes for maximum dramatic effect. The waitress paused, then gave a good hearty laugh, as if she couldn't believe the innuendo came out of the mouth of the grande dame seated before her. She also knew she'd have a good story to tell later.

As soon as we were settled, I got Julie reminiscing about the Persian Room.

"I was wrapping up a show in England when I received word from my manager that I had an offer to open the season at the Persian Room. My English girlfriend from the show, Sally, thought it a grand reason for us to go shopping in Paris, and I had some beautiful couture gowns designed for me by Balmain. Fabulous gowns! The Persian Room was so unique," she continued. "It was a marvelous room, and Ted Straeter's Orchestra played 'The Most Beautiful Girl in the World' every night as I was introduced."

"Many, many great things happened during my engagement there, and I met a lot of wonderful people, but I had one experience that luckily never happened to me again. One night, right at ringside was a couple who had obviously been enjoying their drinks. I was singing my heart out, and the gentleman kept shouting, 'Play "Melancholy Baby"!' This went on all evening long. I told him sweetly that I didn't have the arrangements for that song, but he would not be quiet.

"I thought, my God, what do I do now? I've tried everything I can think of. I really tried to ignore him but he wouldn't stop yelling 'Play "Melancholy Baby"!'—and he was getting drunker and drunker. I thought that maybe if I fussed over him, he'd be satisfied, so I went to his table with my cord and mike and said, 'I'm sorry I can't play your favorite song, but I hope you are having a good time and enjoying your nice dinner anyway. What are you having?' And he said, 'I'll show you what I'm having!' and he tilted his plate toward me until—whoosh! His food just cascaded all over my gown! Steak, gravy, sweet potatoes—all over my dress. My beautiful Balmain *gown*!

"It was probably my own fault for talking to some drunk. Nothing like that has ever happened to me since. And you know what? It ended just as it would in the movies. A man got up from the table across the way and took one of the guy's arms and another man nearby, a large monster of a man, stood up and took his other arm, and they picked him up from his chair and threw him out of the Persian Room and into the marble foyer. With that, I went back to the mike and said, 'Thank you for being such a nice audience. I'm sorry for the disturbance,' and I finished my show.

"Then I went upstairs to my room and cried like a baby! I was so humiliated. The audience was really great, and some lovely man—actually the president of one of the big talent agencies—called me up the next day to congratulate me on my composure. That made everything alright. It had just been one of those nights. You can find scoundrels anywhere, and that night was my turn. I love performing, and the Persian Room was one of the very best places."

With that painful tale out of the way, Julie relaxed and told story after story.

"I used to check out the room in the early evening, before people were seated. It reminded me of a fairyland. Even when the place was empty, it was so magical. The small round tables were draped with double tablecloths, the first skirting the floor and the second artfully arranged over it. The magnificent floral centerpieces made the whole room smell like a garden, scented with roses or whatever was in season at the time. Interestingly, once the room filled with people, the air changed—it began to smell like money! I could smell the expensive, custom-made perfumes and pungent men's colognes from the stage."

Julie and I have become friends, and wherever we go, from coffee shops to the Café Carlyle, she has the same electric effect on people that I witnessed the first time I met her. She still performs at cabarets and clubs around the country, but she tells me she derives particular pleasure and satisfaction from her participation in the International

Before he was world famous as a soloist, Andy Williams
(far left) was a member of the Williams Brothers.

Cabaret Conference at Yale University. It's here at "Cabaret Camp," as Julie calls it, that she gets a chance to meet, teach, inspire, and encourage the next generation of musical performers.

When it's all said and done, Julie'd be the first to say that the Persian Room has a special place in her history.

.   .   .   .   .

PRESIDENT REAGAN PROCLAIMED Andy Williams's voice a national treasure. I'm not about to challenge that assertion, but Andy wasn't always the suave solo crooner that most of us know and adore, and who even now performs to sold-out audiences around the globe.

At the tender age of eight, while in the third grade, Andy joined his three brothers singing in the church choir. They were an instant local hit and started to perform regularly on the radio in nearby Des Moines, Iowa, as the Williams Brothers Quartet. Bob, Don, Dick, and Andy were on a roll, and by 1944, they found themselves backing up Bing Crosby on his hit record "Swinging on a Star."

Soon, the Williams Brothers hit the road, touring the country with Kay Thompson, and it was with her, in 1951 and again in September 1952, that they performed at the Persian Room. Reviewers called the act "trendsetting."

Speaking with Andy, the first thing I wanted to know was, what was so unusual about that "trendsetting" act.

"Well, first of all, we moved around! That probably doesn't sound so groundbreaking, but believe me, it was. Prior to us, nightclub entertainers had traditionally stood in one spot and performed. If there was more than one singer, you all clustered around the microphone the best you could."

"We actually had a choreographer—Bob Alton. So that we could move around more easily, we hung the mikes from the ceiling, and I mean *we* hung the mikes. We actually got up on ladders ourselves and put them where we wanted them, and then we were able to move all over the stage, making our act sort of like a mini musical revue.

"Kay was an enormously dynamic performer. The act she put together was very fast and sophisticated, with high energy and lots of dance movements and singing. Two of our signature numbers were 'It's a Jubilee Time' and 'Pauvre Suzette.' In 'Suzette,' Kay sang, and my brothers and I were at the four corners, harmonizing and dancing around her.

"We were all the same height and wore matching dark blue suits and ties, and as the song was about the men in her life, Kay sang to each of us in turn, injecting different celebrities' names into the skit as her lovers. One she loved 'not enough,' one 'she loved too much,' another 'she loved too often,' and one 'she didn't love.' I was the one she 'loved too much.'

"When she was done singing to me, I fell to the floor,

The uniquely accomplished Kay Thompson first performed
at the Persian Room in 1951 with the Williams Brothers, but
soon brought her solo act there—including her imitation
of a little girl she dreamed up named Eloise.

rolled on my back, and wiggled my feet in the air. It was quite a workout. At the end of the thirty-five-minute show, Kay, my brothers, and I—and the audience—felt like we had performed a full Broadway show."

"We all stayed at the Plaza for the duration of the run, and it was there in the lobby that I was introduced to Stanley Marcus—you know, the cofounder of the Neiman Marcus department stores? He suggested that I take advantage of all the art and culture New York City had to offer, that I should walk and explore and learn from its many galleries and museums. I took his advice and forged a deep appreciation and love for modern art."

That experience clearly set something in motion: Today, Andy Williams is considered a major art collector.

The Williams Brothers and Kay Thompson were booked to open the Persian Room again in September of 1953, but Kay cancelled the engagement. The final appearance of Kay Thompson and the Williams Brothers was on July 23, 1953, in Lake Tahoe.

Soon after the act with Kay Thompson ended, Andy embarked on a solo singing career, and his brothers left to pursue their individual interests. In 1962, Andy was asked to sing the Johnny Mercer and Henry Mancini song "Moon River" at the Oscars, and it swiftly became his signature song. Today he owns, manages, and performs at his Branson, Missouri, club—the Moon River Theater.

. . . . .

KAY THOMPSON CONTINUED to perform, designing
a one-woman act and presenting it at the Persian Room in
January 1954 to mixed response. Unfazed by the reviews,
Kay tweaked the act a bit, changing the format to a two-
person show, with Paul Methuen playing straight man and
butler to Kay's eccentric persona. Kay was back at the Plaza
in November of that same year.

Kay began her career as a vocal coach for radio in the
1930s and was a regular on *The Bing Crosby–Woodbury
Hour* and *The Fred Waring–Ford Dealers Show*. Her big
break came in 1943, when her good friend Hugh Martin
enlisted in the army and recommended her as his replacement as head vocal arranger at MGM. It was there at MGM
that Kay coached singers she would work with for the
length of her career, including Judy Garland and Frank
Sinatra. In 1948, she left MGM to develop her own nightclub act with the Williams Brothers. They made a striking
team that surprised and thrilled audiences across the
country until they disbanded in 1953.

There's no talking about Kay Thompson and Eloise
without talking about Hilary Knight, the celebrated illustrator best known for collaborating with her on the *Eloise*
books. And even better than talking *about* him is talking *to*
him. Hilary may never have played the Persian Room, but
he certainly has warm memories of the many times he sat

in the audience. (And, of course, it is his portrait of Eloise that graces the Plaza lobby to this day.)

Hilary was a gift to me from Kaye Ballard. When I talked to Kaye, she said, "You must talk to Hilary. He knows everything." That led to a treasured friendship, and you know what? Kaye wasn't too far off. Hilary might not know everything, but this born-and-bred New Yorker knows a lot!

With his knack for setting the scene, Hilary suggested we meet in the Plaza's Champagne Court, the spot that was once the Persian Room. It was a superb idea—and not only for communing with the local ghosts; they also serve a fabulous brunch. Hilary ordered eggs Benedict and I had yogurt, berries, and a chocolate croissant—fruit cancels out chocolate, right?

Once we'd taken the edge off our appetites, I knew Hilary was ready to reminisce.

His family moved from Roslyn, Long Island, to Manhattan in 1932. Hilary's parents, Clayton Knight and Katharine Sturges, were commercial artists working in advertising, fashion illustration, and children's books throughout the 1920s, '30s, and '40s. "My own interest from an early age," said Hilary, "was to do exactly the same thing. And I did just that.

"In the late 1930s, my mother took my brother Joey and me to the Algonquin and the Plaza as a special treat. On my own in the '40s, going to the Persian Room, I saw Hildegarde at the peak of her long career.

"In the 1950s, Lisa Kirk hired me to design a serpent

glove she could use in her musical parody of Adam and Eve. But it was an evening in 1954, in that glamorous room, that changed my life forever.

"Living on West 52nd Street, my next-door neighbor was a young lady known as D. D. Dixon, a fashion editor at *Harper's Bazaar*. She later married John Barry Ryan III and became known in theater and society circles as D. D. Ryan—but in those days, she was D. D. Dixon.

"D. D. had met Kay Thompson on a fashion shoot for the magazine with photographer Richard Avedon in 1951. Kay had already made a spectacular nightclub debut with the Williams Brothers in California. In New York, a cabaret was literally created for her called Le Directoire, decorated by William Pahlman, who had previously worked on the Persian Room. Kay and the Williams boys were a sensation—so much so that no act following her succeeded and Le Directoire soon closed.

"Kay had many careers, all successful. She was an exceptional musician, a recording artist, and an arranger and writer for MGM's top musical stars—the likes of Judy Garland, Lena Horne, and Frank Sinatra. With her wicked comic delivery, she entertained her friends over the telephone as a six-year-old she called Eloise. One of the lucky recipients of the comic calls from Eloise was my neighbor D. D. It was her idea that Kay write a book about the mischievous child—and she said she knew the perfect illustrator for the project—me!

"With my portfolio under my arm, I went with D. D.

to one of Kay's final performances at the Persian Room. Within a year, Kay Thompson and Hilary Knight had brand new careers creating the Eloise books!

"Eloise was literally born that night in the Persian Room. My inspirations for her were British cartoonist Ronald Searle and a small British humor magazine by the name of *Lilliput*. My sketches were particularly influenced by Ron's terrible little St. Trinian school girls. They were these horribly ugly little girls in school uniforms, getting into dreadful trouble under the headmistress's nose.

"Kay and I worked side by side, right here at the Plaza. She'd give me little lines like, 'I have a little dog that looks like a cat' and I'd draw. You know, she had an apartment here for a long time.

"Our first book, just called *Eloise*, came out in November of 1955. *Eloise in Paris* came along the following year. For that one we went to Paris twice to soak up the atmosphere. Then came *Eloise's Christmas* and *Eloise in Moscow* and finally we went to Rome for *Eloise Takes a Bawth*."

Eloise turned fifty-five in November 2010 and Hilary is still as enthralled with her as ever. He is constantly asked by bookstores to sign autographs and give talks on her. Last year Hilary generously donated all of his writings and illustrations to the New York Public Library.

Perhaps you think we have wandered away from the subject of night life at the Persian Room, but the spirit of the Plaza in the '50s is present in every wonderful word and

THE

$Persian Room$

Presents the Gala Return of

Lisa Kirk

and her company in a new act
Musical director – PETER MATZ

TED STRAETER
His Songs, Piano
and Orchestra
**MARK MONTE'S
CONTINENTALS**

THE PLAZA
FIFTH AVENUE
AT 59TH STREET
PLaza 9-3000

An ad for one of Lisa Kirk's eight Persian Room appearances. She has described her onstage persona as "a sextrovert without being a sintrovert."

drawing of the Eloise books, so I'm sure you'll agree that it was a worthwhile detour. And since Eloise herself wasn't available for an interview (taking a bawth, no doubt), Hilary made a brilliant substitute. I knew he'd have a lot to say about Kay Thompson, but his vivid memories of Lisa Kirk came as a wonderful surprise.

. . . . .

LISA'S KIRK'S EIGHT appearances at the Persian Room were extraordinary but really weren't planned. Born in Brownsville, Pennsylvania, in 1925, she had been accepted and enrolled to study law at the University of Pittsburgh, when she traveled to New York to keep a friend company as she auditioned for the chorus line at the Versailles nightclub. I don't know if her friend made the cut, but Lisa was offered

Jazz made a brief but memorable appearance at the Persian Room in 1958, when Duke Ellington (far left), Jimmy Rushing (second from left) and a host of other jazz greats assembled at a party hosted by Columbia Records. Lucky for us, the event yielded two albums—one headlined by the Duke and one by Miles Davis.

a place in the line—the back row, but it was a start. College was forgotten, and law was traded for show business.

Lisa gradually migrated from the back row to singing with the band between shows. Soon she was winning small parts in Broadway musicals; the first being *Good Night, Ladies* in 1945. It was in the 1947 production of Rodgers and Hammerstein's *Allegro*, singing "The Gentleman is

Billie Holiday and John Coltrane were also on hand for the Persian Room's brief foray into jazz.

a Dope," that she became a real Broadway presence. The next year she had the lead role in Cole Porter's *Kiss Me Kate*. After a year and a half, she handed it off to none other than Julie Wilson.

During Lisa's eighth cabaret show at the Persian Room, she was flanked by four dancing and singing boys, billed as the Four Saints. MGM records was so enthusiastic about the show that, with the assistance of the popular musical director Don Pippin, it was recorded and released as *Lisa Kirk at the Plaza*.

Hilary spoke admiringly of Lisa. "She was a great performer, wonderful looking with a terrific voice. You know, when they made the movie of *Gypsy* with Rosalind Russell, it was Lisa's voice singing, not Rosalind's. And her husband, Bob Wells, wrote the 'Eloise' song for Kay."

In past interviews Lisa described her style as "sextrovert" without being a "sintrovert." "A sextrovert is a girl who's sexy, but not in an obviously naughty way. The minute you get obvious, you're being a 'sintrovert,' and that isn't good."

After her huge stage success in *Kiss Me Kate* in 1948, she spent forty years entertaining in the Persian Room and other nightclubs, on Broadway, and in films, including *Here's Love*; *Me Jack, You Jill*; Jerry Herman's *Mack and Mabel*; Mel Brooks's 1968 film *The Producers*; and Noel Coward's *Design for Living*.

Lisa passed away on November 11, 1990, at sixty-five, from lung cancer, although she didn't smoke. Some say it was all of that secondhand smoke she inhaled while entertaining in nightclubs, but we'll never know.

·　　·　　·　　·　　·

LISA KIRK WASN'T the only performer recorded live at the Persian Room. The high-class supper club snapped to a new beat when jazz arrived in September 1958, in the form of Miles Davis, Billie Holiday, Jimmy Rushing, and Duke Ellington.

The aforementioned greats assembled at a party hosted by Columbia Records, and the recording of the event was not intended as anything more than a souvenir. But the sounds were too bracing, too edgy, too scorchingly hot *not* to share with the public. The party lasted into the early morning, and the result was not one but two albums. *The Miles Davis Sextet–Jazz at the Plaza* featured Miles Davis, John Coltrane, Julian Adderley, Bill Evans, Paul Chambers, and Jimmy Cobb. Duke Ellington, Billie Holiday, and Jimmy Rushing were showcased on *Duke Ellington and His Orchestra–Jazz at the Plaza.* Was it a new era for the Persian Room? Not really, but it was certainly a once-in-a-lifetime moment.

.   .   .   .   .

ANOTHER LADY WHO is still as lively as ever is the great Polly Bergen. Before the reminiscing began, she patiently explained the nightclub scene hierarchy of the 1950s to me. "The Copa was the big, big star place to play. That's where Frank Sinatra played." (Frank also played the Persian Room, but we'll get to that further down the road.) "It was rather like Vegas East Coast: big draws, big money, in a very commercial hotel. There was the Empire Room in the Waldorf Astoria, but that was a terrible room, and people didn't like to play it.

"Then there was the Persian Room, and it was the most

beautiful room to play in the world. The Plaza was a selective venue. It was almost square, and the orchestra and the stage—well, it really wasn't a stage but the area where we sang—was in one point of the square and when you sang you were looking out to the three other points. It was a totally clear, perfect place to play; you could see everyone, and they could see you. It was not small but still very intimate in the way it was placed."

Polly became a household name through her numerous and varied stage and television appearances. She costarred with Gregory Peck and Robert Mitchum in the very dramatic *Cape Fear* and again with Mitchum, almost twenty years later, in *The Winds of War* and *War and Rememberance* (garnering Emmy nominations in the process). My favorite Polly moments are her comedic turns in *Move Over, Darling*, with Doris Day and James Garner, and the 1964 *Kisses for My President*, where she portrayed the first female president of the United States. (We're all still waiting to see that happen for real.)

Although Polly has been recognized for her acting, when I asked her if she had to pick a favorite talent, she quickly replied singing. She started out as a singer, on radio and in small venues from the age of fourteen, and that opened doors to acting.

A few years later, and after studying math in community college, Polly attracted the attention of Hal Wallis, the legendary movie producer. Wallis is probably best known for producing *Casablanca* and winning an Academy Award for it, but that is just one in a very extensive line of significant movies he produced. He was nominated a whopping sixteen times for Oscars and seven times for Golden Globes. He won two Golden Globes for Best Picture and was honored with the Cecil B. DeMille Award for lifetime achievement in 1975.

I was dying to find out how the two met.

"I was playing a small club, and at that point I didn't have an agent or manager or anybody," Polly said. "Clarence Freed came in, heard me sing, and said he'd like to handle my career. I said, 'Great. Fine.' And Clarence sent a picture of me and a recording to all the well-known producers in Hollywood. I had just recorded a wild hillbilly song: 'Honky Tonking.' The picture was a very glamorous shot of me in a low-cut dress with my hair swept to one side and long rhinestone earrings. So here was this very sophisticated-looking girl and this honky tonk song.

"One of the producers he sent it to was Hal Wallis, and he was kind of mesmerized. He asked me to come in. I met him, and he signed me that same day. He put me in my first three movies—with Martin and Lewis." Those films were *At War with the Army*, *That's My Boy*, and *The Stooge*.

"I adored Dean Martin more than life itself, and I always played his wife or girlfriend, but I had a very hard time with Jerry." What was the friction there? I asked. "Jerry really wanted to screw anybody he worked with, and that was just the way it was. Jerry made my life a living hell, because I wouldn't play ball with him. Every day on the set was so horrendous that I finally walked away. He would just not take 'no' for an answer!"

Polly did a few movies, including *Escape from Fort Bravo* and *Cry of the Haunted*, and then focused on her singing, taking her act to Vegas and the Persian Room in New York.

"At the Persian Room I did a Helen Morgan medley in my act." Helen Morgan had been a troubled but talented torch singer, known for draping herself over the top of a piano and crooning her blues straight from the heart. She died at the age of forty-one.

"That was really something. I was under contract to MGM, and they were going to do *The Helen Morgan Story*. When I heard that, I went to meet with Mervyn LeRoy, who was a big time producer at MGM, and I tried to convince him I should play it. He explained that I was way too young to play that part—and I was—but I also didn't have enough experience. It got me started putting this medley together because, when I looked into her story, I found out she was this incredible torch singer, and that was the music I loved to sing. I became fascinated with her and immediately put her music into my act. As a matter of fact I closed my act with it. It was a tremendous asset in the show.

"So, I had just finished my act in the Persian Room, and all the sudden I get a call from downstairs that there was a little old woman who'd like to come up and see me. I said,

'Who is she?' And they said, 'She's Helen Morgan's mother.' I said, 'Oh, my God.'

"She came up, and she was this little old lady. She sat down and explained how moved she had been by the medley I had done. We started talking about Helen, and during the conversation I told her how badly I had wanted to play the part, but Warner Brothers had already bought the film rights, and they were going to do the film. 'Well you know,' she said, 'no one's bought the television rights.' I said, 'No kidding?'

"So right then and there I bought the television rights. I paid twice what they paid for the movie rights—they stole those. I immediately sat down and started getting as much information from her as I could. Then I hired a writer to write the script.

"Now, all of this was on my own. I hadn't sold it to anyone. I was paying for it and hiring writers and all that. Then I went out and tried to sell it, and no one would buy it because they didn't think it was interesting, and they didn't think my name was big enough to carry a television show like that on my own."

"They were probably right, but I kept trying and trying, and finally I decided I'd just sell it, and they wouldn't have to cast me in it. Just so I could get some of my money back. I had well over a million dollars invested in it. About that time *Playhouse 90* was being produced by a friend of mine, Martin Manulis, and I called him and talked to him about it. He said, 'Let me see who I can get interested.' And he piqued the interest of George Roy Hill, who went on become a very famous director. They then sold it to *Playhouse 90* on CBS and went looking for someone to play Helen. There wasn't anyone around who both acted and sang. There just weren't any acting singers. So I lucked into playing it. That's how it ended up on the air.

"That was the mid-1950s. I played the Persian Room a few times more; the last time was in 1965 with Sandler and Young, and that was the last time I ever sang on stage. I retired from singing after my last show at the Persian Room and concentrated on acting. With *Morgan* I played a very dramatic role, and it was that show that made me a name. [And it won her an Emmy Award.] It was then that I became known as a dramatic actor.

"One of my fondest memories of the Persian Room was the night that David O. Selznick was in the audience. After the show I received a handwritten note from him that said, 'Tonight a star is born.' He never hired me for one of his films, but that note was inspirational."

These days, Polly is doing lots more than sitting around reminiscing. She has a recurring role on *Desperate Housewives*, which she says is " great fun." She played a recurring role on *The Sopranos* and starred in the 2001 Broadway revival of *Follies*. "Just last month I sang for a charity event that Phyllis Newman put together. I was a little nervous, but once I started singing 'The Party's Over,' a theme song of mine, I felt like I did at twenty. My voice was pretty good."

. . . . .

DIAHANN CARROLL ALSO turned one of her performances at the Persian Room into a record: *The Persian
Room Presents Diahann Carroll.* The recording was
supervised by Don Costa, the act staged by Phil Moore, and
Peter Matz led the orchestra.

At age ten, Diahann, born Carol Diann Johnson in the
Bronx, received a scholarship from the Metropolitan Opera
and started learning the fundamentals of singing and performing at the High School of Music and Art. During that
same time, she modeled for various Johnson Publication
magazines including *Ebony* and *Jet.* After high school she
enrolled at New York University with the intent of studying
sociology, but the allure of entertaining couldn't compete
with sitting in a classroom.

After winning the TV talent competition *Chance of a
Lifetime* three weeks in a row, she left with $3,000 and a
singing engagement at the Latin Quarter. She was just seventeen years old.

Diahann's Broadway debut was in Truman Capote's
1954 *House of Flowers.* In 1962 she earned a Tony Award
for her performance in the Richard Rodgers musical *No
Strings.* She made her film debut in *Carmen Jones,* and
in 1968 she was the first African-American actress to star
in her own television series, *Julia,* for which she won a
Golden Globe.

When we met, Diahann and I chitchatted about the

Diahann Carroll poses with recording mogul Clive Davis.

weather, and the transition from East Coast to West. Then we got down to business.

"I remember having my very first meeting about the possibility of my appearance at the Persian Room. I think maybe there had been one other Afro-American female prior to my arrival. From the tinkling glasses and the china and beautiful room, it was exciting on so many levels. It was a thrill to stand offstage and hear the orchestra strike up the band, knowing it was time to go on and do my show.

"In 1959 I didn't have a choreographer. In those days, it was stand in front of the microphone and sing. Later came choreographers."

Jule Styne, the famed songwriter and lyricist, attended Diahann's opening night at the Persian Room and was clearly impressed. "This beautiful, fragile, delicately feminine young women singing 'Heat Wave' made us believe in her, as the most dangerous *femme terrible* became a lyrical, wistful maiden in love singing 'Misty,' and a charming child-woman singing 'Goody, Goody.' It was a *total* performance. She became all these personalities, and we in the audience believed in her."

Diahann's first song of the night was "Everything's Coming Up Roses," which just so happens to be a very popular Jule Styne song.

"I can't help but notice," I mentioned, "the difference in the ads the Persian Room put out in 1959 and then in 1961 and 1963. In the 1959 ad, you looked very sweet and all wide-eyed, but then *very* sophisticated a few years later."

"In 1959 I was at a very young place. Good God—1959! I was working all the time and felt very fortunate to have that in my life. I was married—fairly recently married. It was a wonderful time for me personally because I was married to Monte Kay, a very caring person who was invested in the work I was learning to do.

"I had a baby in 1960 and was a working mother. My husband and I were trying to have a family life. I had no idea what I had gotten into there. I thought it was easily done."

"You were ahead of your time," I noted. During the '60s, women were just starting to think we could do it all.

"I don't know how any of us did it. I entertained in the suite—we had nightly cocktail parties—and the hotel was wonderful about that because we had some unbelievable people who came to see the show. The Kennedys came, Judy Garland, Josephine Baker came a few times—just everyone. It was just a glass of champagne after the show with friends who came to say hello.

"I worked at the Persian Room on and off for nine years, and it was always a very exciting time for everyone. The move into the Plaza included my family, toys, nanny, and assistants as well as music, all there for the big move!

"One thing I remember very clearly is that after my daughter reached a certain age we learned to use the Plaza hallways as a park, because very often it was snowing or storming out. Suzanne and I played baseball in 'our' park—the hall. We would take the baseball bat and softball and play. It was safe because there weren't any windows to break. The hotel hallways were very large, so we had a good practice area.

"My daughter was named by the entire staff the 'Black Eloise of the Plaza.' It was wonderful because she could

In these ads for Diahann Carroll's shows of the late '50s and early
'60s, you can see the evolution of her look from sweet to sophisticated.

move all over the hotel. There was a period when even her cat lived there. Everyone made her feel so at home. It was her home, and she thought it was her house! She was too young for pranks, but she did skip all over the lobby."

In wrapping up our conversation, Diahann shared that at one time she thought the Plaza the perfect spot to commit suicide.

What?!

"It was really adorable because I took one sleeping pill and a bottle of Cristal champagne and went to the Plaza to kill myself. I think I knew I was playing a game. But I wanted a certain gentleman to feel very remorseful about how he had treated me. My friend who went with me—to the Plaza to kill myself—was my neighbor, Mrs. Miles Davis."

"Who was the gentleman who treated you so poorly?" I asked.

"You noticed I left that out! Well, all the champagne did was make us giggle. We fell asleep, and the next morning we woke up, had a beautiful breakfast, and left the hotel."

In the 1980s Diahann stirred up trouble weekly as Dominique Deveraux on *Dynasty* and later its spin-off, *The Colbys*. Speaking strictly for myself, I tuned in weekly, not knowing if I'd love or hate Dominique's shenanigans but always knowing I'd covet the wonderful Nolan Miller costumes she'd be wearing.

Diahann is famous for looking fabulous, and even fashion critic Richard Blackwell, who was sparing (to say the least) in his praise, called Diahann "possibly the most perfect woman" and included her on his best-dressed list often.

On April 21, 2010, Diahann gave a live concert to benefit the Annenberg Theater at the Palm Springs Art Museum. The one-woman show has been shown numerous times on PBS as part of its fund-raising programs. Fans can also catch Diahann in a reccuring role on the USA Network series *White Collar.*

. . . . .

BY 1957, THIRTY-NINE million American households had a television, and most of them were tuned to *American Bandstand,* hosted by Dick Clark. He was delivering recording stars right into our living rooms and we loved it. The first song he played nationally was Jerry Lee Lewis's "Whole Lotta Shaking Going On," and his first guests were Billy Williams and the Chordettes.

The Academy Awards were televised for the first time in 1953, when Audrey Hepburn got the Best Actress award for *Roman Holiday,* and Best Picture went to *From Here to Eternity.* The Grammys were inaugurated in 1958, with Best Male Performance honors going to Perry Como for "Catch a Falling Star." Ella Fitzgerald owned Best Female for *Ella Fitzgerald Sings the Irving Berlin Songbook.*

The end result of all the media exposure was the drive to see our favorite stars in person, in nightclubs, and supper clubs. And that was very good news for the Persian Room.

Some other wonderful Persian Room
performers from the 1950s:

Edith Adams

Count Basie

Gilbert Becaud

George Burns and Gracie Allen

Mindy Carson

Carol Channing

Wally Cox

Pierre and Anna D'Angelo

Jane Froman

Genevieve

Bob Hope

Burl Ives

Evelyn Knight

Beatrice Kraft and Her Dancers

Elsa Lancaster

Dick LaSalle and Orchestra

Lilo

Denise Lor

Kyle MacDonald

George Maharis

Jana Mason

Mata and Hari

Mary McCarthy

Marie McDonald

Sal Mineo

Mark Monte and His Continentals

Jane Morgan

Katyna Raniere

Johnnie Ray

Mary Raye and Naldi

Reyes and Los Chavales

Lillian Roth

Jean Sablon

Dorothy Shay

Herb Shriner

Yvette

CHAPTER FOUR

The 1960s

When the lights go out all over Broadway, The Plaza glows a little brighter.

The Plaza is New York's blazing late show, a Roman candle at midnight, a sentinel against the dawn.

Conversation crackles in the Palm Court after 8. Wit flashes through the red-velvet underground of Plaza 9-. A late supper warms the Oak Room. The volcano mutters in Trader Vic's. And stars come out in the Persian Room.

Torches have been kindled at The Plaza, hearts set afire, bridges burned. It gives a lovely light.

THE PLAZA

HOTEL CORPORATION OF AMERICA

An ad for the Plaza from the 1960s.

With some seventy million baby boomers reaching adolescence, the decade of the '60s was nothing if not the age of youth. The conservatism of the 1950s gave way, and anything offbeat, radical, and fresh was embraced by a generation eager to shatter the mold set by their parents. It was the era of the counter-culture, a time of political transformation, artistic invention, and social experimentation on a scale never before seen in American history. Women's liberation (abetted by the availability of the Pill), grassroots political action, widespread drug experimentation, and communal living were the more substantial movements afoot. On the style side came bell-bottom jeans and suede jackets, impossibly skimpy miniskirts, long hair for everyone, white leather go-go boots, and a general shift away from the buttoned-down "uniform" of the '50s in favor of a more casual, anything-goes image.

The "Camelot" Kennedy presidency and the momentum of the civil rights movement made Americans start to feel that anything was possible, until a tragic succession of assassinations as well as the fallout from a nasty faraway war brought us all back to earth.

You might assume that the timeless little boîte known as the Persian Room was immune to the effects of those social tidal waves, but make no mistake, things changed there, too. Well... a little bit. Suits replaced tuxedos on stage and in the audience, and short dresses triumphed permanently over evening gowns. As more people commuted in from the suburbs to work, there was often no opportunity to go home and change for a night on the town; business attire became evening wear and has remained so ever since. (More's the pity!)

New York City was the center of the cultural universe the day four shaggy-haired young men stepped off a plane from

Bobbe Norris took a turn on the Persian Room stage in the '60s.

England and revolutionized music forever. On February 7, 1964, the Beatles checked into the Plaza and stayed for five chaotic days, dodging the paparazzi and frenzied fans as they prepared for their inaugural U.S. appearance on *The Ed Sullivan Show.* After that, the sky was the limit for them—and for rock-and-roll.

Back on earth, Persian Room audiences were exposed to a wider variety of stars and top-notch entertainment than anyone imagined possible. Broadway superstars, pop singers, uproariously funny comedians, mystifying magicians—all had their moment on the jewel box stage.

·　·　·　·　·

CONSTANCE TOWERS'S SHOW-BUSINESS career has been a superb blend of extraordinary talent, extreme good luck, and perfect timing.

While still in drama school, Connie was strolling down Fifth Avenue with Ben Lipset, a friend who happened to be a talent agent, when they ran into Pierre Boultinck, manager of the St. Regis Hotel. After introductions, Pierre asked Connie if she could sing. She looked to Ben...

"Yes, she can sing," he quickly confirmed.

"Can you open in three weeks at the Maisonette in the St. Regis?" he asked. Another act had cancelled, and he needed someone to fill the spot.

And so it began.

On opening night at the Maisonette, Max Arno, head of casting for Columbia Pictures, was so dazzled by Connie's performance that two weeks later she found herself jetting off to Hollywood to sign a contract with Columbia Studios. Her movie career was off and running when she costarred with Frankie Laine in Blake Edwards's *Bring Your Smile* (1955).

Young and eager to work, Connie decided things were not moving as fast as she'd hoped in California. She moved

Constance Towers was in her early twenties when she first performed at the Persian Room.

back to New York and resumed her singing career, stepping right back onto the stage of the Maisonette. This time, she was spotted by producer Marty Rackin, who pursued her for a film he was making with John Wayne and William Holden, directed by John Ford. (It seems Connie had to be in New York to get the attention of Hollywood.) So back she went to California, for her first big movie, *The Horse Soldiers* (1959), followed quickly by Ford's *Sergeant Rutledge* (1960).

If they'd offered frequent flyer miles in those days, Connie would have cornered the market. After she wrapped the Westerns, in 1961, she returned to the New York cabaret scene, this time performing at the Persian Room.

After a few more movies, she added Broadway credits to her enviable resume, debuting in 1965, at the Ziegfield Theater, in the title role of Anastasia in the play *Anya*. Connie went on to play Anna opposite Yul Brynner in *The King and I* for an amazing eight hundred shows. She also won the New York Outer Critics Circle award for her portrayal of Maria in *The Sound of Music* in 1967.

But wait, there's more. In addition to the movies, theater, and nightclubs, Connie appeared in countless television shows, even playing leading roles on the soap operas *Capitol* and *General Hospital.* She's guested on *Frasier, Baywatch, Criminal Minds, The 4400, Star Trek, The Fresh Prince of Bel-Air*, and myriad other television series.

I caught up with Connie at the beautiful Beverly Hills home she shares with her husband John Gavin, a businessman, actor, and former ambassador to Mexico. I couldn't wait to ask her about her wide-ranging career and the stellar success she enjoyed at such a tender age.

"I was around twenty-three when I first played the Persian Room," she told me. "The Plaza was wonderful. It had such glamour. There was a sparkle about that hotel that made you feel good when you were there. My show was basically show tunes, just like cabaret today—Gershwin or Cole Porter or Richard Rodgers. There were four back-up singers and the Ted Straeter Orchestra.

"As part of performing there, you had a beautiful suite where you could entertain people after the show, and I took full advantage of it. I had Joan Crawford over once! It was a Sunday night, and I was planning to go out with my friends Al and Dorothy Strassard, when the phone rang and a wonderful voice said, 'Miss Towers? Please hold for Al Strassard.'

"When Al got on the phone I said, 'That is quite a secretary you have.'

"'Don't you know who that is?' he said—he was laughing. 'It's *Joan Crawford* darling!'

"I had just finished making *The Horse Soldiers* and had seen Joan in Las Vegas, at a party. I was so in awe of her, I said to a friend, 'Isn't she beautiful?' I don't know how or why but apparently Joan thought I said, 'My, she's gotten older.' Well! I never thought that and certainly would never have said it. Apparently Joan told the Strassards, our mutual friends, that she had been so insulted that I, this young actress, had commented on her age. Later, when we were all in New York, they told me about it and I said, 'My gosh, I didn't say that! Oh, please bring her to my show at the Persian Room!'

"I walked out, and Joan was sitting ringside, wearing a very ornate, very tall orange Balinese beaded hat and matching coat. When my twinkle lights came on, she twinkled twice as much as I did! Oh, she loved being the center of attention. She was on a double date, along with Spyros Skouras, the head of Twentieth Century-Fox. Every time Joan's date watched me for more than a few seconds, she pulled out a cigarette and held it up so that he would have to turn away from me to light it for her. She must have had fifty cigarettes during my show—and this was ringside, where everyone in the room could watch. It was rather fascinating, actually.

"After the show, they all came upstairs to my suite. There was a couch and a chair and she stayed in the corner of the couch and never said a word. She just stared at me. I was standing by the door when they got up to leave. She took my hand and said, 'I have to have tea with you. I have been very mistaken about something. I will call you tomorrow, and my car will pick you up at three.'"

"I didn't have other plans, but if I had, I would have cancelled them because who would miss the chance to visit with Miss Crawford?

"Sure enough, she sent her car at the appointed hour—a Rolls-Royce—and the chauffeur drove me to her apartment, which was up on Fifth Avenue somewhere in the Seventies. When I arrived, Joan was busy giving an interview, but when the reporter left she showed me around her apartment, a fabulous triplex overlooking Central Park. Then we went downstairs, had tea, and she apologized.

"I was in awe of the whole experience. I finally had a chance to tell her myself that what I had said was how beautiful I thought she was. I guess she believed me!"

Nudging Connie's attention back to the Persian Room, I asked her if she'd had a choreographer for her shows there.

"I had a man by the name of John Gregory who did my shows, and he was a genius—just wonderful. I always relied on him. My shows were about fifty minutes long. I'd always change my gown for the second show, and I'd try to change the music as well, or at least the sequence of the numbers, because there were some people who would come multiple times, maybe one night for the first show and another for the second."

Since I'd mentioned her gowns, Connie asked if I'd like to see one. I sure would!

These particular gowns were designed by the movie director Mitch Leisen and had been commented on by reviewers because they were so extraordinary. They were referred to as *string* or *fringe* gowns and cost around $10,000 in 1961! Connie still has two of them.

"I don't know what to do with them. I can still wear them and hate to just give them away, although I did give the white string gown away. At one point my singing teacher told me about a girl who was opening someplace and needed a gown. I said I have something I think would be right. I gave her that one but I still have the red one and the green one. Let's go take a look."

With that Connie and I entered the walk-in closet off her bedroom, and she showed me the most beautiful dress I have ever seen. I really understand why it was so costly. Connie explained that each piece of string had to be measured and placed just so to conform to the shape of your body. The dress and all the draping was done with pieces of silk string.

What a perfect ending to a wonderful day.

.   .   .   .   .

VISITING MICHELE LEE, I found it impossible to believe that almost fifty years had passed since she'd starred alongside Robert Morse and Rudy Vallee in *How to Succeed in Business Without Really Trying*. Michele greeted me at her beautiful Beverly Hills home looking vivacious and fit. She was wearing black tights, a long-sleeved black T-shirt, and ballet flats—as if she'd just stepped out of rehearsal or off the set of her 1969 Walt Disney hit *The Love Bug*.

Michele's television and screen career took many forms and crisscrossed different genres, including roles in Carl Reiner's *The Comic* (1969), in which she starred with Dick Van Dyke and Mickey Rooney, and the musical production of *Roberta* (1969). In 1996, Michele made history when she became the first woman to write, direct, produce, and

*Singer and pianist Buddy Greco, who contributed some
of the musical arrangements for Michele Lee's Persian
Room debut, congratulates her after the show.*

star in a television movie called *Color Me Perfect*, the
story of a mentally challenged woman who is used in a
scientific experiment to reverse her disability. Returning
to Broadway theater, she received a Tony nomination in
1974 for her performance in *Seesaw*, the Michael Bennett,
Cy Coleman, and Dorothy Fields musical adaptation of
William Gibson's *Two for the Seesaw*.

But none of that made Michele a household name. That came in 1979, when she took on the role of Karen Cooper Fairgate in *Knots Landing,* a TV spin-off of the popular nighttime drama *Dallas. Knots Landing* dominated prime-time ratings until 1993, running an impressive 344 episodes—and Emmy-nominated Michele set a record by appearing in every single one.

According to Michele, her entire family was musical. Her father was a Hollywood make-up artist who loved the piano and also wrote songs, one of which, "What a Day," was sung by Jimmy Durante.

As a teenager, her brother, Kenneth Dusick, played guitar and dabbled in song writing, and Michele even wrote a few with him. And the tradition continues: Kenneth's son Ryan, Michele's nephew, is one of the founding members of the successful rock band Maroon 5.

Squinting and trying to capture titles from Michele's substantial CD collection, located in the corner of her spacious great room, I asked Michele if she always knew she wanted to be in show business.

"My mother always said I sang in my crib," she laughed. "I sang all through school and in junior high I was known as 'the Singer.' I started singing quasi-professionally when I was sixteen, with a society band. We performed on weekends, and it was thrilling to get paid for what I'd always done for fun!

"While I was still underage, I lied so I could work in LA,

at a club called Dino's on the Sunset Strip. As a matter of fact, the building Dino's was located in was used in the hit television series, *77 Sunset Strip*."

I turned the conversation to Michele's memories of New York and the Persian Room. How did she come to perform there, I asked her.

"I had an incredible manager, Stanley Kay. Before he was in management he was a drummer for Buddy Rich, and he was a brilliant, funny, magical musician. Anyway, he arranged for me to audition at the Persian Room. I had already done *How To Succeed in Business Without Really Trying*, and I think I had also just completed the movie– but I had to audition because I was an unknown quantity outside of stage and screen. That was the real beginning of my singing and nightclub career. I had done a little singing in Los Angeles, but this was big stuff. To sing at the Persian Room meant you'd made it. You'd *made it* in New York!

"My audition consisted of twenty minutes of my act, me and a pianist, and they hired me. I performed there twice– taking my act to the Sands Hotel in Vegas in between."

At that point, Michele's wonderful executive assistant, Tina, brought us coffee–though it tasted more like heaven: freshly ground with foamy, sweet heavy cream, sprinkled with sugar, and accompanied by cinnamon sticks. She also brought us strawberries, grapes, cheeses, and yummy bis-cuits to keep us going. Who wants to work? I thought. I just want to sit here and lose myself in Michele's gracious hospitality, while enjoying the view of the golf course and the LA canyons out of her floor-to-ceiling windows.

After a little break, I asked Michele if any well-known people had come to see her perform at the Persian Room.

"Diahann Carroll came to see me. All I remember is that something went wrong; I forgot a lyric or something. She was really hot stuff then—a big star. She was Diahann Carroll and didn't have to audition anymore! Knowing she was there must've made me nervous. The notes came fast, and the words came fast, and I got so hung up that I don't think I ever caught up. All the while I was thinking, 'Oh my God, Diahann Carroll is out there!'"

Later, talking with Diahann, I asked her if she remembered Michele's flub. " No, I don't remember that at all. Michele Lee was always a very strong and interesting performer. She always did wonderful work."

Michele continued telling me who was there for the show. "Jim Farentino was my husband at the time, so of course, he was there. David and Ellie Janssen and Paul and Peggy Burke were our good friends—they were there. David was a huge star because of *The Fugitive*, and Paul was in a hit TV series *The Naked City*. Other pals of ours who came included Jerry and Marta Orbach, Buddy and Dani Greco, and Harry and Patty Duke Falk. They were all part of our 'gang.'

"Buddy Greco did some charts for my act, just as a friend. I believe the song was "On the Other Side of the Tracks." I think it was my opening number.

AHB160 (34)(08)BB499
B AMA286 PD FAX AM NEWYORK NY 26 333P EDT
MISS MICHELE LEE
  CARE PLAZA HOTEL SUITE 1670 FIFTH AVE & 59 ST NYK
ALL THE LOVE I HAVE GOES WITH YOU TONIGHT. BE BRILLIANT, HONEST
AND GET PREGNANT LOVE
  JIMMY
(00).

On the day of her Persian Room opening, Michele Lee received this telegram from her then husband, James Farentino. (They were waiting to find out if she was expecting a child at the time.)

"At that time, I was with Columbia Records and had a hit record with 'L. David Sloane.' I was always working on something. Those years were all about career, career, and career. Well, I guess not completely. I remember I was trying to get pregnant during my Persian Room run. Talk about working all night, then up all night! At that time, if you thought you were pregnant, you had to go through this whole test and you waited forever for the results. It didn't happen until the following year."

Figuring it might be time to change the subject a little, I asked Michele about what she liked to wear for her act. It was, after all, a time when just about anything went, fashionwise.

"I wore some great dresses," she told me, her eyes lighting up, "but one of my favorites was a dressy miniskirt in some kind of shiny gold fabric. I don't remember the designer, but it was sleeveless, with a really cool bronze, hand-beaded and jeweled metal collar. The dress was backless except for very delicate, metal crisscross straps that came from the neckpiece, down below my waist and just above my... um... you know what. It was very sexy.

"After the show, we'd either entertain or hang out with friends. Many times Marta and Jerry Orbach had everyone over to their place. They lived downtown and had a huge wooden kitchen table. Marta would cook, and the gang would all sit around, tell stories, eat pasta, and drink wine. Fun times."

. . . . .

GOING OFF TO visit with Tony Butala, the founder of the fabulously popular singing group the Lettermen, felt like a real adventure, so I decided to share it with Sabrina and Marina. After a bus ride from New York's Port Authority to New Jersey, a quick visit with my mother (who loves to pamper all three of us with the home cooking we rarely get in the city), and a visit to the local farm stand for Jersey corn and tomatoes, it was off to Lancaster, Pennsylvania. That's where Tony and the Lettermen—still going strong— were giving a concert at the American Music Theater. Tony had kindly carved out a slice of time to tell me what the Persian Room was like when the Lettermen played there.

As I drove through rural Pennsylvania, watching the beautiful scenery fly by, I was mentally reviewing my notes on Tony and the Lettermen. The three-hour trip passed quickly, and soon I was sitting in the lobby of the Hampton Inn, our meeting spot, nervous that I wouldn't recognize Tony. Those worries were put to rest when a very handsome silver-haired man stepped off the elevator, only to be enveloped by fans who'd come to town especially for the concert. When the hubbub subsided a bit, I sidled over and introduced myself, and we made our way to a corner table at the cheery hotel restaurant. I knew I'd have to work fast, as Tony was soon due at a sound check with the rest of the group.

He started out the conversation by volunteering his age—seventy! You'd never guess it, believe me.

"I've been with the Lettermen fifty years and singing professionally since 1946—sixty-four years. I still love it," he said. Wow, only six years old when he started. I asked him how that came about.

"Okay, here's the long and short of it, probably more like the long of it. I was five and a half years old, living in Sharon, Pennsylvania, and I didn't want to go to school. The first day, my parents couldn't find me. Eventually they did, two fields over, on top of the highest tree. When they finally got me to go, I clowned around and disrupted the class. I just had too much energy.

"So my mother enrolled me in dance class. I was the only boy with all these girls. In the '40s, ballet was a sissy thing to do, and I got teased for it—but I thought those guys were nuts because even at five and a half I thought girls were great. I was in heaven: thirty little girls and me!

"The teacher had a dance recital to show the parents where their twenty-five cents a month went. As the only boy, I was a star—I played Johnny Jump Up and I stopped the show! Our phone started to ring off the hook: the Moose Hall, the Elks, the Knights of Columbus, the Rotary Club, all asking for little Anthony to do their Christmas Party or Fourth of July bash, and sure enough, I went.

"There seemed to be an aversion to paying kids money. They'd pay the piano player five dollars but give me a set of cuff links or a watermelon in the summer. I was six years old and my mother looked in my little drawer and saw thirty-five sets of cuff links. So we started charging five dollars. Another year went by, and in the second recital I had five numbers. My fee went to ten dollars after that and then fifteen dollars.

"KDKA radio in Pittsburgh was the first commercial broadcasting station in the world. Once a month, I'd go down there and do the Saturday morning live program. I was heard in Ohio, Pennsylvania, Indiana, Michigan, New York, and many, many other states. So my fame spread, and

I was getting calls to do shows as far away as Rochester, New York. I was getting about twenty-five then. That was more money than my dad made."

Enthralled by Tony's story, I didn't notice it at first, but a throng of his fans had gathered at a discreet distance, hoping to catch Tony's eye. We paused briefly so a few could introduce themselves. Tony chatted graciously with Stacey from Detroit, Melva from Cleveland, and others. After a few minutes, he dismissed them gently so he could get back to his story.

"One day, my mother got a call from her cousin in LA. Mary Burke was her name. She had pneumonia and couldn't get her kids ready for school, and her husband was off working on an oil derrick. My sister looked up the train schedule. 'Tomorrow morning, at eight, you can catch the Phoebe Snow from Sharon, and you'll be in Los Angeles in three days and two nights,' she told my mom. My dad said, 'Why don't you take Anthony with you? Maybe he can sing for someone.'

"As it turned out, every fall Bob Mitchell had auditions for new kids for his choir; as the old ones grew up they had to leave because their voices changed. My cousin Bobby auditioned and was told, 'don't call us we'll call you.' Then it was my turn. I gave Vince Morton, the assistant director, my charts and started in, trying to hide my nerves. In a few seconds, he got on the intercom and said, 'Bob, you better see this kid now.'

"So, at ten I became a member of the Bob Mitchell Boys

Choir in Hollywood. Bob had his own boardinghouse and school, and the kids got paid. My mom cried all the way home, but within two years my family moved out there. I was doing movies and becoming successful."

Hmm, time was passing and we were only up to Tony, age twelve! The truth is, I could've listened to Tony forever, but I knew I'd better fastforward to the '60s. We weren't quite at the Persian Room yet, though. The mention of that decade got Tony talking about his good friendship with Sammy Davis Jr.

"I first met Sammy when I was with a lounge group, Bill Norvas and the Upstarts. We were three guys and two beautiful girls. This was in Vegas, and Sammy would come and watch us after he did his two shows. We had the late shows, 12 a.m. to 5 a.m., and Sammy rarely slept, plus, he liked one of the girls, Laurie Mattis. We had a lot of good times in Vegas. After the Lettermen's first hit, Sammy suggested I take on Jess Rand as my personal manager. It was Jessie who got us the Persian Room, Jess and our theatrical agent, William Morris."

I asked him my favorite question—did he get nervous, especially performing at a swanky place like the Persian Room?

"As a matter of fact, we were nervous about playing the Plaza—but Jack Benny—whose TV show we'd been on, and who had taken us on tour—came to our rescue. He happened to be working in New York the week we opened and offered to introduce us. Jack was a big star, and he knew that a place like the Persian Room could make us or break us. No matter how many hits we had, we'd have to have a good show. Well, we knew we had a good show. Peggy Lee and Sammy and all the Capitol Records people said they'd be there, too, which boosted our confidence.

"At the last minute Jack couldn't make it. Instead, he sent a tape recording of his introduction the morning of our opening: 'Ladies and Gentlemen, I'm sorry I can't be there with you tonight but I'd like to introduce three men who have toured with me and been on my television show. They're spectacular. Ladies and gentlemen—the Lettermen!'

"He managed to get there a few days later and introduce us in person, but for the rest of the run, we used his recording to let people know we had some credentials. I mean, he *was* the number-one television star in the world.

"Then it was our turn. We came out, well dressed, engaged the audience, sang wonderful songs, and had a great act."

Tony was fully engaged in telling stories and probably could have gone on and on, but I had to insist we take a short break so I could make him some hot raspberry tea. His concert was in just a few short hours, and I wanted him to conserve his voice for all of those adoring fans. When he'd taken a few sips, he continued.

"Judy Garland came to see us at the Persian Room. We had met her when Sammy had us out to Paramount Studios in Brooklyn to tape a special. We tended to hang out at Danny's Hideaway on Lexington and Fifty-second, where a lot of celebrities went."

Even more than the Who's Who in the audience, I was curious about the act itself.

"We always wore tuxedos. Sy Devore was our tux maker. He made tuxes for Sinatra, Dean Martin, Sammy, everyone of taste. If you had a Sy Devore tuxedo, man—wow. People could tell by the cut. Even though tuxedos sort of look alike, these were the best. I still have them.

"The show was natural in flow and movement. We'd go out into the audience. In those days there were only corded mikes, so we had to figure it out carefully: okay, if I reach the center, I pick up another mike and go this way or that way. And sometimes we'd end up with a lot of spaghetti on stage.

"I didn't want to be the kind of group that was aloof from the crowd. I wanted to tell the audience that after the show we would be out in the lobby signing autographs. Jess said, 'Ah, Tony, I don't think the Plaza will like that.' And I said, 'why not?' Sure enough, those sophisticated ladies and gentlemen loved it. Our job was to loosen them up, help them relax and enjoy themselves.

"We included audience participation in our act, in the form of a 'camera song.' We'd say, 'Ladies and gentlemen, if you brought a camera along tonight, take it out.' This was groundbreaking—people weren't used to taking pictures during performances. We actually asked people to sing along and have their pictures taken with us. We got one man to be Elvis. We'd get a lady to sing and bump to 'Won't you come home Bill Bailey, won't you come home.' We weren't sure this stuff would work at the Persian Room, but you know what? It worked fine! People just want to have a good time. We still do it all in our act today, but we broke it in at the Persian Room in the '60s! In fact, our camera song was so well received that it inspired the Plaza to hire a house photographer to go around and take pictures of couples.

"Those days were just the greatest time in the world. Everyone dressed up. You couldn't walk into a restaurant without a tie. I loved it. Things were more special then. You'd see people enjoying tea in the Palm Court in the afternoon, all the ladies dressed up in their finest outfits and gloves. It was an elegant time. The audience respected the performers, but the performers also had the greatest respect for their audience. You dressed as well or better than your audience because they were paying to see you."

The concert that night was fantastic—it lasted two-and-a-half hours, and the crowd still wanted more. The Lettermen proved they still had magic, closing to three standing ovations!

.   .   .   .   .

BETTY JOHNSON WAS the one and only performer I spoke to who had a cherished love story to share from the Persian Room. Her name might not be instantly familiar, but Betty is a bona fide performer. She was launched into show business as a young child, touring the country and recording albums for Columbia Records with her family,

Once she's enticed him to come up from the audience,

Betty Johnson's brother Kenneth joins her in a duet.

the Johnson Family Singers. Eventually, she captured the top spot on the *Arthur Godfrey Talent Scouts* show and, with the guidance of Percy Faith, branched out on her own, with much success, I might add.

At a Columbia recording session with her family, Betty first met Percy Faith. They were getting ready to sing "The Halleluiah Train" when she noticed a slight man enter the control room and sit down to listen.

"I was curious as to who he was and quickly found out he was a famous Canadian conductor and arranger, and he'd just joined Columbia to work with the big names— Tony Bennett and Rosemary Clooney, among others.

"At that initial meeting he presented me with an album of Jerome Kern's that he had just produced. I took the album home and memorized every single song."

When Betty wrote a note to Faith, thanking him for the wonderful album, he responded with other recordings and became a teacher to her, helping her craft her style and hone her music choices. He sent her classical albums that developed her tastes in a new direction and offered to help if she ever decided to pursue her solo dreams in New York.

"Percy Faith was my mentor and helped me find and navigate the path I needed to go."

He introduced her to the New York music scene and helped her transition from a southern traditional singer into a popular music performer.

After scoring the top spot on *Arthur Godfrey Talent Scouts* with her redition of Irving Berlin's "How Deep Is the

Ocean," she was featured for a week on his morning show. The exposure she received was explosive. She was on a swift path to entertaining in the most posh New York night-clubs, starting with an invitation to sing at the Copacabana.

"In 1957, Jack Paar was in the audience when I appeared on *The Ed Sullivan Show*. I sang my hit "I Dreamed," and he told me later that he'd decided to hire me on the spot, but he didn't tell me then because other singers were still audition-ing. I got the job and was a regular on *The Jack Paar Show* for four happy years, singing in the first and last segments.

"That exposure brought me many other bookings. That's how I got the Persian Room booking.

"I encountered the love of my life, Arthur Gray Jr., while I was performing in Los Angeles at the Coconut Grove. I dreamed of him every day and was anxious to pursue a relationship, but he lived in New York. The Plaza offered that opportunity. Each night, Arthur was in the audience with a table full of friends, all very attractive people. After the performance he'd ask me over to meet them, and then just the two of us would go to the Oak Room. I was in heaven.

"My dress was white chiffon with a beaded top, designed by Oleg Cassini. I felt very attractive because the lighting in the room was pink and soft and dramatic with a sophistica-tion that most rooms lacked.

"In later years, I didn't perform there, but I did go to the Persian Room as Mrs. Arthur Gray Jr. On one occasion

Robert Goulet introduced me by telling the audience we had played together in *Brigadoon* and asked me to take a bow."

Betty and I hadn't talked in awhile, so I called her at home in Bliss Tavern, New Hampshire, where her recording company Bliss Tavern Music is also headquartered, to see how she was. I was profoundly saddened to learn that Arthur had died suddenly, after a successful knee replacement. She told me wistfully, "My strongest memory of the Persian Room is that Arthur and I were in love, not married yet, and he came to hear me sing every night. Of course, I sang every song on the program to him. Afterward, at the Oak Room, everyone knew him, and we had chicken sandwiches and champagne."

.   .   .   .   .

CATHRYN KENZEL'S STORY is different because she entertained at the Persian Room in 1968, when she was only fifteen years old. "I was very, very young. When most people played that room they were already big stars, but my story was different. The Persian Room gave me my start.

"I started singing at age three and was very fortunate because I had a great gift and two fanatically supportive parents who were thrilled that I wanted to sing, and wanted me to succeed as much as I did. I was brought up in a show biz family, so singing and performing was something I was very accustomed to and comfortable with. They owned

Cathryn Kenzel was only fifteen years old when she made her Persian Room debut. Here she is with her mother, who put together her shows and traveled with her until she was past twenty; and Tony Bennett, whom she opened for on many occasions.

Ron-Cris, a recording company. Where most parents would say 'grow up and be a doctor,' no, no, no—with my family it was music, music, music. It was an unbelievable experience growing up. My parents handled the Five Satins, and when I was a little kid I met the Four Seasons.

"It was just me and my brother. They were very encouraging and did anything and everything they could to get me a break. You know—network, network and network— and one person led us to another and to another. Someone led us to Joseph Arcana, who was at that time the president of the New York City musicians union. When my parents met him, I was fifteen and ready to burst out.

"He heard me sing and from that point connected me with a lot of different places and people. The Persian Room gig was the kickoff to the promotion of my record *Other Lips*."

Joseph Arcana was a good friend to have because the unions held a tremendous—*tremendous*—amount of power in New York in the 1960s. On his suggestion alone to the Plaza management, Cathryn didn't even have to audition to perform at the prestigious venue.

"I went by Cathryn Rondina at that time, my maiden name. My mother put together my shows, and we opened at the Plaza with 'Get Ready.' It had been done by the Temptations and then redone by Tom Jones. That was my theme song: 'Get ready 'cause here I come.' It was my mother's idea because I was new, I was fresh, I was a kid—and I was ready. I did a lot of Broadway and Streisand songs. I didn't sound like her, but I had a big, belting voice. You could hear me blocks away. At the Persian Room I sang a lot of songs that were powerhouses.

"Vikki Carr was scheduled to appear there the day after I left. She didn't come to my show, but I saw her walk through the hotel. I was so impressed just seeing her. Even at fifteen, I knew what it was like to want to be a star. I was terrified and excited. I don't know, though, if I realized the importance of where I was singing at the time. I knew it was important but maybe not as much as if I had been twenty-five. But maybe that was a good thing because I had no fear. Vikki's manager came to my show because someone told him, 'you should go hear this kid who's playing downstairs.'

"There was a man who worked with my parents in Connecticut, and he was so proud that I was going to perform at the Plaza that he bought me a bottle of perfume from Tiffany's as a good-luck gift before I went on. The reason he picked Tiffany's was because the box was the color of my dress. That's how I remember my dress color!"

Cathryn had been young and sheltered at the time. She told me that her parents traveled with her because she wasn't even old enough to drive. I asked her if the famous Persian Room had lived up to her expectations.

"I've sung all over the United States and in Europe, and I would have to say there wasn't another room that size that was as posh and classy. But that was the hotel. My God, I can't say any place was richer and more elaborate than the Plaza and the Persian Room. There is no other place that holds the same history as that room."

As Cathryn said, she was just starting her professional career, and she didn't have a large following to entertain, so after the show she and her parents celebrated at what could be called New York City's first theme restaurant: Mama Leone's. "It's closed now but was a famous spot. Now

I love Carmines! You can tell I'm Italian. After the Persian Room, my parents traveled with me for about six years."

"I know you sang with many very famous stars. What was it like working with Tony Bennett?" I asked.

"I opened for Tony, and he was wonderful. I remember one day he watched my rehearsal, and I was doing a song called 'Let Me Try Again.' If you are a Sinatra fan you know the song. It didn't become a big hit, but we loved it. Well, Tony said to me, 'Why are you singing a Frank Sinatra song on a Tony Bennett show?' I said, because you're already doing 'I Left My Heart in San Francisco.' We both laughed over that. He was the most funny, charming, great guy out of all the people I met in show business, very honest and down to earth. He said to me 'don't ever be with anyone who doesn't think you're the best thing since ice cream.'

"Rodney Dangerfield was also a very nice guy. He didn't make it until he was older, and I think because of that he appreciated stardom. Maybe you don't as much if you're famous very young and don't have the struggles that Rodney had. After I opened for him at the Oakdale Musical Theater, he booked me for Dangerfield's in New York."

In her early twenties, Cathryn finally went on the road without her parents. She toured all over the United States and at twenty-six, tired of her gypsy life, she went home to Conneticut, where she met her husband and had her daughter. In 1979, she opened a voice studio in Branford, Connecticut, where she combined both her experience and expertise in music with her love of being a mother. Thirty years later she is still instrumental in launching students on their singing and entertainment careers.

. . . . .

COUNTLESS PEOPLE FAIL to look beyond Connie Stevens's arresting beauty and miss the fact that she is a genuine renaissance woman. She's probably best known for her four-year stint as ditzy nightclub singer and photographer Cricket Blake in the 1960s TV detective series *Hawaiian Eye*, but that was just one credit in a long and impressive career as both a singer and actress. At age sixteen, while still in high school, Connie helped formed a singing group called the Foremost, but her time with them was brief; soon she was ready to pursue a solo career. (The other three members of that group went on to make pop history as the Lettermen!)

After winning a role in *Rock-A-Bye-Baby* with Jerry Lewis, she signed a contract with Warner Brothers and has been a staple of TV and the movies ever since. She has also been recognized for her tireless efforts on behalf of America's servicemen. At first entertaining with Bob Hope and the USO, Connie soon struck out on her own to visit and perform at military bases and hospitals around the world throughout the Vietnam and Persian Gulf Wars. For her selfless work and devotion she was awarded the Decoration for Distinguished Civilian Service by the U.S. Army.

Connie Stevens met her future husband Eddie Fisher
while performing at the Persian Room.

As if acting, singing, and charitable work weren't enough to fill up a few lifetimes, Connie raised two daughters on her own and started a beauty empire called Forever Spring, which she markets on the Home Shopping Network. The company has been such a phenomenal sensation that she is considered one of the top five hundred female executives in the United States.

Connie also writes, directs, and produces films and documentaries that have special significance to her. She was gracious enough to invite me to her home to talk the day before she was heading out to Missouri for the premiere of her film *Saving Grace B. Jones*.

At my first mention of the Persian Room, Connie started right in.

"It was—gosh—the late '60s. It was a fun, hip time. I was very young, and the younger crowd was really taking over in places like the Persian Room. If I had to put it into one word, I'd say my act was *athletic*. I was all over that stage. I danced and mimed and sang popular songs. And went from one set right into the next.

"Oh, my God!" she added, laughing as it dawned on her. "I remember the men in my horn section all wore toupees. And I know this because—again—my act was very lively; I moved from this end of the stage to that end and back, and the music was fast and the poor guys were up and down and standing and sitting, playing their instruments. I mean, it was a workout! Well, at the end of the show I looked at the guys and it was some scene. They were all worn out, with their hair pieces cockeyed and askew! I felt bad for them, but they were a great horn section.

"I was a lot younger than the guys in the band. Joe Layton put the show together for me, although there wasn't much choreography because the space you had to perform in was pretty small."

I couldn't imagine that she'd done all of that leaping around in an evening gown—so I asked her.

"You're right there. I wore pantsuits. Michael Travis did my costumes, and they were mainly pantsuits.

"Between shows, I usually grabbed a little something to eat and then got a dinner after the last performance. I didn't eat before the first show. I didn't really do anything special, just reviewed the song sequence, did my makeup, and got dressed. Although..."—and at this point I saw a strange twinkle in her eye—"one time, I had been busy and didn't do my nails earlier in the day; so I was dressed and ready to go and still had time, and I made the great mistake of polishing my nails. I say great mistake because I was wearing one of my favorite outfits, a black top with feathered bell bottoms. The pants had these fabulously beautiful little black feathers all over. A million black feathers. Well, I was on stage doing my act—all happy—sashaying around as usual, and I looked at my hands and the nails were covered in black feathers! I hadn't given them enough time to dry, and with all the dancing around, the wet nail polish

Look out for the sweet young sting!

It's Leslie Uggams. And she has it. And what's more, she's going to prove it in front of everybody in the Persian Room from December 18 until January 7. She's quite a bombshell. When she sings, firecrackers go out of style. She smiles and...what's the use. You'll just have to see for yourself. And speaking of spectacles, Rome is *way out*. Emil Coleman's Orchestra and Mark Monte's Continentals are *in!* For reservations, please call PLaza 9-3000. And for a very lovely evening, visit the Persian Room.

HOTEL CORPORATION OF AMERICA **THE PLAZA**

Leslie Uggams made her television debut at age six,

so by the time she debuted at the Persian Room at

age nineteen, she was a very pretty veteran.

had grabbed the feathers and glued them on. I'm sure that anybody who noticed thought I had done it intentionally— and come to think of it, it wouldn't be a bad idea!

"I met Eddie [Fisher] while I was performing at the Persian Room. We had met before but hadn't gone out because our schedules conflicted. Well, this time we went out, got married, got divorced, and I had my two girls with him."

.   .   .   .   .

LESLIE UGGAMS APPEARED on the TV series *Beulah* in 1950, when she was just six years old. By the time she was seven, she was opening at the famed Apollo Theater in Harlem for such greats as the Louis Armstrong and Ella Fitzgerald. Leslie attended the New York Professional Children's School and then the prestigious Juilliard School, all while maintaining a presence on television and stage.

Just shy of turning fifteen, Leslie became a contestant on the popular game show, *Name That Tune*, where she not only won $25,000 but caught the attention of Mitch Miller. He gave her a spot on his show *Sing Along With Mitch* and signed her to a recording contract. This was groundbreaking: Leslie became the first female singer to join Miller's troupe and one of the first African-American entertainers to become a regular on a prime-time TV show.

Leslie left Juilliard in 1963, making the first of her three appearances at the Persian Room that same year. She was one of the youngest performers ever to play there, and at the time was described as part Lena Horne and part Shirley Temple.

I couldn't wait to ask her how it felt to play the Persian Room at the tender age of twenty.

"The Plaza was such an elegant hotel. I was so young that my mother stayed with me the first time I performed there. During the day, I rehearsed and taped *Sing Along With Mitch,* then I did my show at night. It was an enchanting time—my first nightclub gig, and I was enjoying every bit of it!"

I had to phrase it carefully, but I wondered if young Leslie didn't find the place a little bit stuffy, a little too grown-up?

"Not at all. The room itself was very warm, almost intimate, and the audience was attentive. It was a very welcoming place. This was 1963, and even my Afro-American family was made to feel very comfortable when they came to see me perform.

"The management had such high standards. I was given a beautiful suite for the duration of my stay so I could dress and prepare for my show in pleasant, relaxed surroundings. In fact, I think maybe my own standards became too high because they were based on how the Plaza treated the talent. I soon found out it was not the same at other nightclubs.

"What really stands out in my memory is that I was hired to perform for New Year's Eve. The original plan was for my family to come watch the show and ring in the New

The Persian Room announces a 28-day cruise with Tony Sandler and Ralph Young, who will be duo-ing what comes internationally from October 18 till November 14. Ports of call include faraway lyrics with sweet sounding names.

Burt Farber and Mark Monte will help you sail around the dance floor.

For deck chairs, PL 9-3000.

THE PLAZA
HOTEL CORPORATION OF AMERICA

Tony Sandler and Ralph Young's first appearance at the Persian Room was in the company of Polly Bergen—but by 1966, they were headliners playing to sold out crowds.

Year with me after the show. I also invited a few—anyway, it seemed like a few—other people who didn't have previous plans to join us. Well, word spread, and it became a huge party. My suite was so packed, we had to open the door and people stood around in the hallway. Millions of people! I didn't even know a lot of them. I actually walked into my bathroom, and there were two complete strangers making out in my bathtub! All in all, though, it was a wonderful party. For years and years, I'd run into people and they'd say 'I remember that great New Year's Eve party you had at the Plaza.'"

Recently, Leslie has been busy portraying Lena Horne in a musical bioplay called *Stormy Weather*, as well as performing concerts around the world. I was lucky enough to hear her sing at the Carlyle Hotel (with Julie Wilson as my date) and found myself hypnotized by her beautiful renderings of pop classics, interspersed with stories of her eventful youth.

·   ·   ·   ·   ·

TONY SANDLER USES different words describing his childhood years in West Flanders: innocent, peaceful, playful, and charming. All are meant to portray his young years in the small French-Belgium border town of Lauwe where he, his seven siblings, and his father enjoyed a bucolic lifestyle, engaging in the day-to-day chores of planting crops and tilling the soil on the family farm.

Tragically, Tony was only seven years old when, on May 28, 1940, after resisting for three weeks against insurmountable odds, Belgium surrendered to Germany. Returning to their house, after fleeing in a panic with only a few belongings, the family found their home damaged but still standing. Only days later, a German soldier was quartered in their house for the four-year duration of the occupation.

When life returned to normal and the war ended, Tony was invited to sing with an international choir, and his life-long love of performing was born. His first recording, at eighteen, was a Belgian seventy-eight single, which, translated, was called "The Song of the Sea." Many other records followed, Tony's popularity soared, and requests for concerts followed. After serving in the army in Korea, Tony resumed his performing schedule and quickly became a celebrity.

Tony's smooth, romantic sound rapidly endeared him to European and English audiences alike. But, Tony said, it was the Café Roma, on the Italian Riviera, that he called home for five years. While appearing there, the American producer Frederick Apcar persuaded Tony to appear with the American singer Ralph Young. The next stop for Tony and Ralph and the mainly European cast was the Casino de Paris show at the Dunes Hotel in Las Vegas.

Ultimately billing themselves as Sandler and Young, they soon caught the attention of Phil Silvers, who told his audiences in the main room, "I don't know what the rest of

Patti Page played the Persian Room three times, and drew a somewhat younger and hipper crowd than some of her fellow artists.

you are doing now, but I'm going to the lounge to listen to that hot new duo, Sandler and Young."

"Almost around the same time, Polly Bergen saw our show and asked us to flank her at the Desert Inn in Las Vegas. In 1965, we traveled with her when she took her show to the Persian Room in the Plaza Hotel! That was a big deal to us. By this time Ralph and I had performed in many places, both separately and as Sandler and Young, but the Persian Room had a worldwide reputation of class."

When I asked Polly Bergen about the fact that Sandler and Young were the only performers she ever shared a stage with, she said, "They were *definitely* not backup singers. They were very talented guys. I saw them and felt I just had to have them with me. So I brought them on, and they were a big asset. I thought of them as part of the act and used them as part of the act. They did their own numbers, and then we did numbers together, like duets or trios. They were wonderful."

"We had a fabulous time in Polly's show. After that, we toured on our own, and a year later, in 1966, we were back at the Persian Room but this time it was *starring* Sandler and Young, sold-out shows!"

·   ·   ·   ·   ·

PERHAPS WE HAVE Patti Page to thank when we're stuck in snail's-pace traffic along scenic Route 6A through Cape Cod. Such is her power as a singer that her renderings of "Old Cape Cod" and "Tennessee Waltz" have had a demonstrable impact on home sales and tourism in Massachusetts and Tennessee! In 1967, Massachusetts House Speaker John Davoren and Treasurer Robert Crane presented her with an official State Citation for the contributions to that state's economy. "Tennessee Waltz" had sold more singles by the mid-1960s than any other previous song.

Although Patti was getting ready to leave for a concert tour to the Philippines, she was kind enough to invite me to her picturesque Rancho Santa Fe home to discuss memories of her nightclub years. After a delightful house tour that included a stroll through her office, where scores of platinum and gold records were on display, we sat down to talk.

Patti Page received a set of doorknobs from the Plaza as a gift, after she joked that it was kind of them to welcome her with her own monogram on the doors!

I told her that "Old Cape Cod" had always been one of my favorite songs. "Mine too," she admitted, perhaps not surprisingly. "Claire Rothrock wrote the song, and she lived on Cape Cod. She and the gentleman who published it came to see me when I was playing Blinstrub's in Boston. He played it for me, and I fell in love with it. We made arrangements to go to New York City the very next day and record it."

Knowing that Patti's time was precious, I got right down to business, and asked her how many times she'd played the Persian Room. "Three different times," she told me. "I remember once the Plaza was in the middle of a major spring cleaning. Everything was being polished and refurbished. The hotel manager was showing me around, and we walked into a room that was empty except for piles of doorknobs and switch plates that had been removed and stacked for cleaning. They all had that familiar ꟼP monogram beautifully scrolled on them. I joked to the manager that they didn't have to go to the trouble of putting my initials on the doorknobs! And, wouldn't you know it? The sweet man had one mounted and he presented it to me before I left. You might have noticed it when we went through my office. I still display it.

"My engagements at the Persian Room were a bit different from other people's. I didn't get the crowd that usually goes to the Plaza, you know, the upper-crusty clientele? My audience was classy but not typical. They were a little more country, more hip, and younger.

"I always wore white on stage because no matter

what kind of lights they have in a club, white shows you off well, and you can do a lot with it. That was one of my then-husband Charlie O'Curran's contributions to my act. He also staged it for me—he was a choreographer. He incorporated a glittering, mirrored disco globe overhead that reflected all the lights.

"By the time the show was over, it was midnight. I always ate after the show. Room service at the Plaza ran twenty-four hours a day, so I'd order dinner sent up to the room. It wasn't like when I played Vegas. After the show there, I'd have dinner and then play tennis—until 4 a.m., sometimes. You know, when you're young, you don't even think of the time. I'd go to bed at five, get up at one, and start all over."

Maybe I was getting a little tired of hearing every artist rave endlessly about the Plaza; I asked Patti if she'd had any less-than-perfect experiences there.

"Well, this wasn't the Plaza's fault," she replied, "but there was a giant snowstorm one of the times I was there, one of the worst the city had had in quite a while. Then again—it really turned out for the best. A lot of people staying at the hotel were stranded inside for days with nothing to do, so they came to see my show. The same people came over and over and over. A lot of the employees had to stay, too, and they came to hear me sing. I had packed houses.

"There are certain feelings you get in certain rooms in New York City, and you just know it's the place to be. The Persian Room was one of those rooms. It lent itself to the show and had a warm feeling to it. Plus—it was right next door to Bergdorf's!

"I had five musicians in addition to the hotel orchestra, a hairdresser, sometimes a secretary, my manager, husband—quite an entourage, and that was before I started bringing the kids along. And the management was nice to all of them."

.   .   .   .   .

CAROL LAWRENCE BECAME famous for her dazzling Broadway portrayal of Maria in Leonard Bernstein's *West Side Story*. She cemented her reputation as a singer and dancer starring in many, many Broadway shows, including *Sugar Babies*, *I Do! I Do!*, and *Sweet Charity*.

In addition to being a star of the first magnitude, Carol is one of the most gracious women I've ever met. She had just returned from a tour and had plans for the evening, yet she made time to visit with me on a Sunday afternoon. Not only that, but when I arrived at her stunning home I was greeted with a tempting array of treats: chocolates, exotic nibbles, delicate Italian cookies that I couldn't stop myself from finishing, and sweet hand-squeezed lemonade.

Both Carol and I thought our conversation would be shorter than it was—but when she started replaying events, I noticed a relaxed, playful look take hold behind her eyes. She really enjoyed reminiscing about her New York City

Carol Lawrence shares a joke with her then husband, Robert Goulet.

nightclub adventures! Carol made it to her evening soirée on time—but with very little to spare.

I started out by reminding her that Ed Sullivan had called her Persian Room act the greatest nightclub act he had ever seen.

"That was the headline, and the next day you couldn't get in," she remembered. "We were sold out for the whole run!

"I always say Tony Charmoli, my choreographer and friend for many, many years, was the king of making ladies look great onstage. My act consisted of two boys—Johnny Harmon and Bobby Lane—plus me and a ten-foot-high ladder. I like starting a show 'in trouble.' It started dimly lit, with two spots doing the gangbuster, lights-moving, searching kind of a Dick Tracy look. The music was unidentifiable. Our backs were to the audience and I was dressed as one of the boys because we were pretending that one didn't make it to opening night. The tuxedo purposely didn't fit me well—the sleeves came below my fingers. My long black hair was up under a derby hat. Finally, the orchestra leader said, 'Here she comes...bop, bop, bop. Here she comes... dat, dat, dat...Missss Carolll Lawrrrrence.' We were on our knees looking upstage, and the spotlights converged on an empty space. There was a hush as the audience wondered where I was.

"I was playing Johnny, and at this point, Bobby would take my hat off and my hair would fall out. 'What are you doing in Johnny's tuxedo?' he'd ask.

"I'd say 'You know how Johnny is always late for everything? Well, he's late for opening night! And Mr. John starts the show at eight whether I'm here or not. So I figured I'd just dance his part and sing my part until he got here.'

"He said, 'Do you think it will work?'

"I said, 'We don't have a choice. Hit it maestro!' And we began the song 'I'd Do Anything' from *Oliver*. Right then, Johnny came in, and gave this wonderful excuse for being late—that he was calling his mother. She lived in Florida and he was a real momma's boy, so the whole premise rang absolutely true. I pretended to be all annoyed and said, 'I don't want to hear any more excuses, let's start from the beginning.' I handed him his derby, and the orchestra started the intro again, while I ducked behind a little black velvet curtain where my secretary ripped off the velcro tuxedo. Underneath it was my white leotard, over which I put a fabulous chiffon Ginger Rodgers skirt, a beaded jacket—and ran back on! I changed, came out, said hi, and started my first number in less than thirty seconds.

"We didn't have an opening act. The show was one hour, ten minutes. I told Tony, 'You really choreographed this for Sonny Liston, but he's not here, and I'm dying!'"

I asked her about her most memorable experience at the Persian Room, and her eyes lit up.

"My biggest thrill was...Well, Mr. John always gave me a list of who would be in the audience, so I could point them out. He'd say, 'You must introduce him first and then this one, because he will get angry if he's not first' And on and on. He knew everyone so well. He got tips from all the celebrities to put them at the best tables.

"This time he said, 'Tonight... tonight, tonight, tonight, you are so lucky. He seldom comes, but guess who is here? Cary Grant! But you are not allowed to mention his name because he will not stand up. He will sit at the table closest to the door by my station. He doesn't want to be mobbed. He will not sign autographs. Tonight he is a private person.'

Golden moments in Plaza history (clockwise, from top left):
Dinah Shore rehearses. The incomparable Hildegarde chats with with
Mr. Seay, the Plaza's publicity director, and Mrs. Clarke Williams.
Eartha Kitt knocks 'em dead. Ethel Merman chats with Lucille Ball
and her husband Gary Morton after her Persian Room opening.

"All during the show I saw people walking and moving around and finally I realized what it was. Women would go all the way across the room to the powder room because they spotted him. They would just stare at him all the way over and all the way back. At least they weren't asking for autographs, because if they tried, Mr. John would step in and say, 'No, you are disturbing the show; you must move on.' He really ruled the place.

"So, on that particular night I introduced everyone else in the audience and then—I just couldn't stop myself. I said, 'and of course everyone in the audience knows there is an elephant here who cannot be introduced, but he needs no introduction. I have been a great fan of his from the time I can remember.'

"Cary stood up. 'Well, this just doesn't happen!' he said and I thought he was furious! He folded his napkin—I thought he was going to leave—but he walked to the front and the audience just stood. He came on stage and HE KISSED ME!"

"He said, 'Miss Lawrence...'"

"My knees really almost buckled. I said, 'You are absolutely gorgeous,' in my best Fanny Brice voice.

"'Well, thank you, my darling, and right back at you,' he twinkled. The audience was blown away.

"After the show he came up to my suite and talked with us for an hour. My two little boys, gay as twits, just sat on the floor awestruck. Before he left, I took him aside and said, 'Tell me your secret. You're not twenty-nine anymore,

Ed Sullivan called Carol Lawrence's Persian
Room act the greatest he had ever seen.

but you sure look it. Your skin is exquisite; tell us just one of your secrets.'

"'Well my darling,' he said, 'I sleep a lot. Make sure you get enough sleep.' Oh, he was adorable—such an aura about him.

"The only one to come close to him was JFK. I had lunch with him at the White House. I was in the Oval Office just two days before he was killed, for a press conference kicking off his reelection campaign. Lena Horne was there and a lot of people from Broadway.

"Lyndon Johnson had seen my act at the Persian Room, but I wasn't allowed to introduce him either, for security reasons. He sat in the corner and loved the act.

"We were all going to do a big, big show for the start of his campaign. I was the first of our group to go into the president's office. He shook my hand and said, 'Lyndon tells me you have the greatest act in the world. I can't wait to see it at Madison Square Garden.'"

As big a star as she was, it must've felt pretty special to have the president looking forward to your act.

Other wonderful Persian Room
performers from the 1960s:

Ed Ames
Nancy Ames
Susan Barrett
The Barry Sisters
Shirley Bassey
Cilla Black
Vikki Carr
Xavier Cugat
Vic Damone
John Davidson
Johnny Desmond
Sacha Distel
Phil Ford and Mimi Hines
Sergio Franchi
Jacqueline François
Robert Goulet
John Gray
Tammy Grimes
Sam Hamilton
Noel Harrison
Fran Jeffries
Jack Jones
Kitty Kallen
Alice and Ellen Kessler

Eartha Kitt

Abbe Lane

Julius LaRosa

Denise Lor

Gloria Loring

Dorothy Loudon

Grace Markay

Tony Martin

Gail Martin

The McGuire Sisters

Barbara McNair

Ethel Merman

Liza Minnelli

Matt Monro

Phyllis Newman

Bobbe Norris

Russel Nype

Jane Powell

Juliet Prowse

Katyna Raniere

Felicia Sanders

Dinah Shore
Frank Sinatra
Kay Starr
Enzo Stuarti
Caterina Valente
Monique Van Vooren
Shani Wallis
Izumi Yukimura

CHAPTER FIVE

The 1970s

Peter Duchin follows in his father's footsteps
at the Persian Room piano.

It was in the '70s that we said
good-bye to Elvis and witnessed
the breakup of the Beatles, yet no
other decade saw the launch of
more diverse musical styles and
artists. We enjoyed heavy metal,
soft rock, punk, and pop, and
thrilled to the ballads and pop
tunes of Stevie Wonder, Billy Joel,
Marvin Gaye, and Elton John.
But the single, decade-defining

craze in music was sparked when John Travolta pointed one finger skyward, resplendent in his iconic white suit in *Saturday Night Fever.*

Disco was born, and the country couldn't get enough of the sounds of Donna Summer, the Bee Gees, Gloria Gaynor, and KC and the Sunshine Band. The new sound influenced fashion as well as song and dance: platform shoes, polyester leisure suits, hot pants, Spandex tops, gold-and-white suits that glowed under ultraviolet lights—all became wardrobe staples (on Saturday nights, if not at the office). For the first time in a century, big, bushy sideburns were cool on men. African-Americans proudly displayed huge, round Afros and other natural styles. Farrah Fawcett popularized the feathery haircuts that began replacing the long, straight, center-parted hair of the '60s.

Enormous auditoriums and arenas such as Madison Square Garden, that could accommodate multitudes of screaming fans, became homes for the ground-shaking rock-and-roll performances of the Rolling Stones, Led Zeppelin, the Eagles, Pink Floyd, Chicago, Aerosmith, the Who, and many others. Nightclubs, cabarets, and supper clubs began to fade in popularity, though the flame never went out completely.

The Persian Room greeted the '70s like an elegant, aging dowager, bravely pushing on for another half decade, continuing to showcase the great entertainers of the moment.

.　　.　　.　　.　　.

JUST PRIOR TO meeting me at New York City's Regency Hotel, Lainie Kazan had returned from a trip to England where she visited with friends, had dinner at the House of Lords, and met the Queen at Windsor Castle. I was under no illusion that she would be anticipating our little get together as eagerly as I was—but she seemed genuinely happy to sit down with me and share the American imitation of high tea when the time came.

I had to begin by asking her about her audience with the Queen.

"The whole thing was so surreal," she said, her eyes sparkling with the memory. "We were briefed on how to address her—'Your Highness,' of course—and how to curtsy. She had a brief conversation with each of us. Nothing very important; just weather and stuff. But she drove herself down, in a little car, and came onto the lawn to meet with us."

Lainie had her first huge taste of stardom when, after being Barbra Streisand's understudy in *Funny Girl* for over a year, she got her chance to shine as Fanny Brice for two precious performances when Barbra contracted strep throat. Her reviews in the local press and national magazines were glowing, and Lainie's career was launched.

Over the next almost fifty years, Lainie captivated audiences worldwide as a singer, performing in the finest clubs, concert halls, and Las Vegas clubs. As an actress, Lainie received a Golden Globe nomination for her performance in Richard Benjamin's film *My Favorite Year* and a Tony nomination for the Broadway musical adaptation of the same show. She even picked up an Emmy nomination for her guest spot on the TV show *St. Elsewhere.*

There's lots more to say about Lainie's long and varied career—including the fact that she was the inspiration for Jack Kirby's DC comic book heroine Big Barda—but the point here, after all, is to talk about the time she spent at the Persian Room. The day after Lainie's SRO opening, Robert Alden reported in the *New York Times* that "an audience may have many reactions to Miss Kazan, but they will not ignore her." I wondered what led her to that particular venue.

She warmed to the topic immediately. "I had very recently left *Funny Girl,* and my manager got me into the Plaza. They gave me a summer date because they didn't know if I'd bring in the business, and they were taking less of a risk in summer, when there are fewer people anyway. They didn't pay me much at the beginning.

"After that first booking, I was there three or four times a year for months at a time. Eventually they gave me a suite for the entire year. Anytime I wanted to come to New York I would stay there. It was gorgeous. I had never seen anything like it in my life. They were unbelievable to me. I had the suite Elizabeth Taylor had shared with Richard Burton.

"I thought after that everything would be like this first foray into the cabaret world. Ha!"

"The club was very intimate. Even though it held 250

Lainie Kazan looks positively dangerous in this early publicity photo.

people, it felt smaller. I remember it always being packed. People would stand in line for hours to get in. It was so elegant. On one night alone, in my audience, were Cy Coleman, Ethel Merman, and Joan Fontaine. After the show I'd have friends over to my suite for a glass of wine. We'd sit around or go out to another club. Liza [Minnelli] would come over, and we'd go out. Places were all open very late. I partied hearty—I was like a werewolf!"

I asked her about what she wore for her performances. "Great, great gowns," she told me "made by Ray Aghayan, Bob Mackie's partner. This one gown made me look—at a glance—like I was nude, but I wasn't. It was the color of my skin, had a jeweled buckle, and graced my legs with chiffon. It was gorgeous. I also had many other incredible clothes. I still have some of them in a big trunk.

"Oh, I'll tell you another story," she said, laughing as she remembered it. "I carried my own sound system with me along with my trunks. One of the trunks was an enormous thing that once belonged to Sophie Tucker. Really, really huge. I bought it at a place called Jimmy's Trunks on Ninth or Tenth Avenue. It was black and looked like a coffin. It opened, had a pole, and all my gowns would hang in there. I used to make the doormen and bellmen carry all this stuff to my suite. They'd have to open all the double doors just to get it through. They would see me coming and they would die—that's how I traveled—with the trunks and speakers. Big speakers. I didn't like their sound system so I carried everything.

"They'd say, 'OH, NO, she's coming.'"

I knew that Lainie had performed at the Persian Room in both the '60s and '70s, and I wondered if she'd noticed the club changing with the times.

"Well, here's one thing that could never have happened in the early days of the club. My girlfriend Cynthia was married to a guy, Steven Friedlander, but he called himself 'Brute Force' because he was against the Vietnam War and everything establishment. He wrote songs that were way out of the box—very edgy, very outrageous songs that I thought were brilliant. I said to him, 'Steven, you have to open for me at the Plaza.'

"I don't know if you can write this, but I'm going to tell you because it's one of the great stories of the Persian Room. Eartha Kitt used to come in a lot, and she was there the night that Steven performed. She had come with Liza. All the singers were there. Well, Brute Force walks on stage with his loose, bright red hair flowing halfway down his back. He wears tails, high-top sneakers, no tie, and he sits at the piano and starts to sing."

I think I'll spare you the lyrics Lainie repeated to me, but suffice it to say they were not from the common cabaret lexicon!

"The audience just gasped. Paul Sonnabend, the owner of the hotel, was hysterical. He said to my manager 'Get him off that stage or she's out of here!!' And we had to fire him. Hysterical. It was hysterical. It was the '70s, and I was very irreverent then. I thought it was great, but I guess they

Liza Minnelli and her new husband, Peter Allen, join their good friend Lainie Kazan after her opening-night show.

didn't think it was so great. I never had him back because they threatened to fire me."

When I asked Lainie if there was anything she missed from those days, she said, "I miss the elegance and the dress code. People got all dressed up to come hear you sing. They respected what you were doing. They'd eat and drink before the show—never during it. When you were performing nobody moved! The show was the SHOW. There was always great regard for the artist. I really miss that. When you go to a venue now, some dippy waitress is serving ringside, and you want to kill her. They don't even know what they're doing wrong.

"The Persian Room had a great staff, and we had great, great times. That roomed sizzled. It sizzled!!"

. . . . .

IT'S MY PARTY and I'll cry if I want to, / cry if I want to, / cry if I want to. / You would cry too, / if it happened to you.

The lyrics to Lesley Gore's chart-topping hits swirled nonstop through my head for days leading up to our get-together. She is a singer, songwriter and the most successful solo artist of the "girl group" era. Her first hit, "It's My Party," went to number one on the pop charts while she was still a junior at the Dwight School for Girls in New Jersey. She soon became a platinum-selling pop singer with hits such as, "Judy's Turn to Cry," "You Don't Own Me," "Sunshine," "Lollipops and Rainbows," and "Bobby's Girl."

She also had villainous fun playing Catwoman's evil assistant, Pussycat, on the *Batman* television series in 1967. All this, while simultaneously studying drama and literature full-time at Sarah Lawrence College in Bronxville, New York.

We met at a very good seafood restaurant called Fulton's on the Upper East Side of Manhattan. It was a picture-perfect day, the kind New Yorkers rarely get to enjoy. So we decided to have lunch outside on the small, sunny patio, ringed by lush green potted trees.

I asked Lesley to tell me the first thing that came into her head when she thought about the Persian Room.

"I recall the stage being on the floor level," she said. "You weren't higher than the audience. I really played to the tables. There was a small platform for the band. I say band but it was really an orchestra. I had a rhythm section with ten horns. Another thing I remember about playing the Persian Room was that they didn't have a spotlight. It must have been out of order or something. We needed a dress rehearsal to calculate which ceiling light worked for which songs. After marking the perfect spot, I had to remember to stand exactly there when singing a specific ballad. That was a big deal at the time—a big pain.

I told Lesley that she'd always impressed me as being very calm, very "go with the flow," and asked her to corroborate.

"Well Patty," she said, leaning in for emphasis, "you have

to understand that I was just a kid and didn't really expect or plan on my degree of success. Quincy Jones heard me sing and said I should make a record. So I thought, 'sure, whatever, let's make a record.'

"This is a story that's been told before, but it really exemplifies the time. A more uncomplicated time. Back then, we would book a studio and turn out a record in a day. Now, you're lucky to get it done in a month. Anyway we recorded 'It's My Party' during the day. Then Quincy hosted a party that night and got to talking with Phil Spector.

"Phil told him that a group he was managing, the Crystals, was going to record the best song he ever heard: 'It's My Party'!

"Quincy immediately figured out that we had been 'double dealt' by the publisher. There were two partners, and one sold us the exclusive rights, and the other sold them to Phil Spector! The next day−Sunday−Quincy went to the studio and pressed one hundred copies of our version. It took him all day, but he was able to mail them out on Monday to the biggest radio stations across the country, We preempted Phil's record. Three days from start to distribution! Try that today."

When I asked her how she passed the time when she wasn't performing or recording, Lesley smiled mischievously and said, "I had an apartment in New York City but rarely stayed there. I was dating a new guy, so it was more exciting to stay in the room the Plaza offered rather than either of our apartments. We spent a major portion of my free time in that suite with room service. It was a lot of fun.

"I vaguely remember that the cover charge at the Persian Room was twenty dollars, maybe twenty-five dollars. It wasn't very expensive compared with today. There were a ton of wonderful people in my audiences. I remember Mayor Wagner came one night, so did Diana Ross, Barbra Streisand, Lainie Kazan, Trini Lopez, Little Anthony, and Liza Minnelli—and those are just a few that jump to mind. It was an awesome place that pulled people in. People came no matter who was performing. I'm sure my name brought in certain fans, but the room itself brought people who just loved to come to the Persian Room.

"One of the things I loved about playing there was that the Persian Room enabled me to try new material. I wasn't just a rock-and-roller; I was interested in jazz and other kinds of music, and I put it all into my show. I had the opportunity to do songs other than my hits, and that was satisfying for me. That's what entertainment is about. It was a wonderful experience, possibly one of the best per-forming experiences I've had. I always thought the Persian Room was really the ultimate in clubbing."

Lesley continues to sing, write, and perform. She snagged an Academy Award nomination for cowriting the Top 20 hit "Out Here On My Own" for the soundtrack of the film *Fame*. She also starred in the Broadway musical *Smokey Joe's Cafe* and still entertains millions with her concerts at a variety of venues.

After lunch with Lesley, walking home through the foyer

of the Plaza, I again found myself humming, but this time the song was "I wanna be Bobby's girl,/ I wanna be Bobby's girl, / That's the most important thing to me. / And if I was Bobby's Girl what a faithful, thankful girl I'd be."

.   .   .   .   .

I OWE HARLAN Boll, the prominent Hollywood public relations guru, big time for introducing me to Barbara Van Orden. I hadn't heard of Barbara before Harlan called and told me she opened for Frank Sinatra at the Persian Room and asked if I wanted to speak with her. Not only is Barbara beautiful, funny, talented and nice but she has great clothes. She arrived wearing a fabulous mink vest I immediately coveted.

Barbara and her dishy husband Elton spent an afternoon regaling me with anecdotes of her start in show business, first as a Breck Girl in commercials and then opening for Morey Amsterdam, Buddy Hackett, Shecky Green, Frank Sinatra, and a slew of others before becoming a headliner herself.

Barbara's story is vaguely similar to many Hollywood fairy tales but set in New York City. "My mother and I were at Reicher's restaurant having coffee and pastry. An agent with the Loretta Marshall agency was also there and asked me if I would do a Breck commercial. Mother was very strict and wise, and she said, 'Well, we will see.'"

Shortly after that, they went to his office, and Barbara

was signed to do the commercial. She was sixteen. Breck was followed by Maybelline mascara, Yardley lip gloss, Calgon bath beads, and various voice-overs.

"I was a singing cow for Dorman Cheese—a singing cow! But it paid good money."

Over one hundred commercials later, Barbara pursued what she'd always loved to do and embarked on a singing career. Her first stop was the Catskill Mountains resorts, where she opened for male singers and comics.

"It was great fun. I worked at the Nevele and Grossinger's. Jennie Grossinger would walk around keeping a sharp eye on everything, and she'd say to all the single girls staying sat Grossingers, 'Daahling have I got a boy for you.' Such a matchmaker."

Soon, Barbara was singing at Playboy Clubs. She reminisced, "Boy, I remember those clubs. They were very popular. I did them all" and, beating me to the question by a *hair*, said, "No, I wasn't a bunny!"

Next stop Vegas. "I did a lot of Vegas—when Vegas was Vegas! There were many great entertainers in the show rooms and also great lounge acts. We'd do our show, and afterward we'd all go to the lounge shows.

"Twenty minutes: Every opening act was twenty minutes. The main act might be an hour or so, but the opener was a tight twenty minutes, and it was exciting because you opened for someone terrific and fantastic—big stars. A so-so performer wouldn't have an opener. When I met up with Frank Sinatra in Vegas, I was opening for Shecky

Barbara Van Orden was lucky enough to work with Frank Sinatra until she became a headliner herself. They were lifetime friends.

Green. One night, when I was doing my gig with Shecky at Caesars, Frank came to see the show. Afterward he came back and said, 'Would you like to open for me? I'm going to the Persian Room at the Plaza in New York.' I said yes in a heartbeat.

"Being from the East Coast, I had been to the Plaza a lot: the Palm Court, Trader Vic's, the Oak Bar. Frank had been asked by some 'very special people' to do a private party there. Otherwise I don't know if he would have done it. Who knows? He could be very lovely or not so lovely. And he was very nice and very good to me. I just lucked out.

"I worked with a lot of people, and one was Soupy Sales. One night I was ready to go on and he said to me, 'You know kid, I'd like to hit on you but the word is out.' The Word? I'm thinking what word, what word? Finally, I had the courage to ask, 'Soupy, what word?' He said, 'Well, Frank let it be known that anyone who does anything that he wouldn't approve of with Miss Van Orden would have to answer to him.'

"Ahh. Thank God for 'the word.' A lot of the girl singers would be asked out to dinner by male singers and comedians that they opened for. And guess who was dessert? You guessed it—the girl singer! There was a lot of that kind of thing going on. We would think of all kinds of excuses, any excuse you could possibly think of, to get out of going down that path. But thank God for the gig at the Persian Room and thank God for Frank Sinatra and 'the word!'

"I think it started the night I opened for Frank in the Persian Room. My son was a little boy and he had the flu, and my sister was with him. I was getting dressed and ready to go on, and I was on the phone and asked him, 'Did Aunt Terry give you ginger ale? And he said, 'Yes mom, Aunt Terry gave me ginger ale and read me a story.' At that exact minute Frank was going by my door and hears this. For the longest time he'd say, 'How's our little boy? Is he feeling better? And how is Aunt Terry?' From then on, Frank was very protective.

"I was invited to his place in Palm Springs many times; usually to low-key parties with fellow performers. The parties were absolutely wonderful, the performers supreme and the music the greatest. Under each doorway of the house was a mat with the name of one of his hit songs. He had a great big room with a screen. The parties were absolutely wonderful.

"Up until the time he got ill he'd call now and then, and when I'd answer the phone he'd say, 'How's Aunt Terry' or 'How's our little boy?' and I'd know immediately who it was."

Barbara didn't work with Frank as much as she would have liked to. He was in his later years and didn't work as much as he once did. Besides, Barbara had become something of a main attraction herself!

"When I was working with Frank at the Persian Room, *Fiddler on the Roof* was a smash on Broadway, and the *Exorcist* movie was playing all over town. I thought, hmm, this is too good, I have to write a parody about this. So, I wrote a parody combining *Fiddler* and the *Exorcist*. I came up with: 'Oh, Exorcist, Exorcist, do what you can, put a little devil back in my man' to the tune of 'Matchmaker.'

"I was always trying to figure out how to win over the fellas in the audience. A lot of men were in town for conventions or on business. A female singer can undulate out in a black satin gown with a lot of cleavage, but that only keeps their attention for about a minute and a half. So I thought, why don't I write a parody about the stock market? I did and they loved it."

Originally I wanted to print the words to this very clever limerick but Barbara asked me not to, so you just have to catch her show and I guarantee you'll laugh.

Since her shows sounded like so much fun, I asked her whether anything particularly memorable ever happened during her act. Her eyes twinkled.

"One night, right before the show, I'm thinking to myself, Oh, God, I'm going to open, and Frank doesn't usually have people open for him. How patient will the audience be with me? They really want him! I go out a little nervous. Usually, because I wrote most of my material, I was very comfortable and relaxed—but not that night.

"I had asked Frank whether it was okay if I entered from the back of the room. You checked everything with Frank, at least if you were smart. He said, okay, which was great because that was kind of star stuff. I'm so nervous that I'm shaking going out, thinking 'they want him,' but I tell myself, it's only twenty minutes, I'll do my act and get off.

"I go out, wearing an amazing Nolan Miller black beaded gown, very form fitting with a mermaid tail and a seven-foot white-fox stole, and start moving toward the stage. Cyd Charisse, Tony Martin, and Carol Channing were a few of the greats in the audience. On my way to the stage I would touch certain people in the audience to win them over. The audience was very nice and very receptive. Milton Berle was such a ham, when I took his hand he looked at me and said, 'Hey kid, you don't have palsy, do you?' I guess I was shaking. The audience laughed and I relaxed.

"Then Berle said, 'Kid, you want to work with me?' Everyone was hearing this and laughing, but now I start getting nervous again, thinking maybe Frank will be annoyed because, not only did I enter from the back, but I'm getting laughs! Maybe he just wanted the girl singer to sing her songs and get off. Finally, I get to the stage singing, I look around, the audience is smiling, I feel great! This is a success. I do my *Exorcist* bit and a few ballads, the stock market parody, some up-tempo stuff, and then I'm off—strictly sticking to my twenty minutes.

"Going off, I get nice applause, and Frank's there, ready to go on, and I say, 'Okay?' He says, 'Okay, kid.' And then, bumppa pa bump—the horns start to play and out he comes and the crowd goes wild!!"

When nightclubs started to disappear, Barbara went into the business end of the business. Her personal management company representing writers and producers was located in Culver City, California. She was later invited by Universal Studios to form her own movie production company, Cinequest, and move to the Universal Lot. This she did with her husband writer producer, Stephen Heilpern.

Now, after thirty years of being behind the camera, she's back!

Barbara is currently performing around the country. Critics have written of her high-profile return to the stage, admiring her deep, rich tones; powerful voice; and impeccable comedic timing. Offering audiences entertainment reminiscent of the glory days of Hollywood and Broadway, Ms. Van Orden represents cabaret at its best!

.   .   .   -   .

KAYE BALLARD IS a star of stage, television, and famous nightclubs. She has performed at the White House for President and Mrs. Ronald Reagan, at the London Palladium for the Royal Family, met Mother Teresa, and even seen Marlon Brando naked. I was afraid my interview with the multitalented entertainer, a first-generation Italian, was off to a treacherous start when she inquired at Cuistot, the best classic French restaurant in Palm Desert, California, about their pasta dishes—and they didn't have any. Luckily (for both of us) the chef graciously whipped up a delicious plate of farfalle for her. As we waited for it, a parade of well-wishers drifted up to our table, and Kaye was uniformly kind to them, chatting and patiently signing scraps of paper.

In reviewing her 1975 visit to the Persian Room, *New York Times* columnist John Wilson wrote: " Miss Ballard is a comedian with a sharp sense of timing. A singer with vocal reserves that can rival Ethel Merman's brassy tone. A musician and actress who can project a sentimental attachment to her Italian grandmother so convincingly and winningly, that it becomes an unstoppable climax for her act." He concluded by saying, "Miss Ballard's talents and most important, the warmth of her personality and the believability she projects, even in the midst of clowning, holds it all together." Wow.

As the last of the well-wishers drifted away from our table, we settled back to enjoy our lunch and visit. I broke the ice by asking about where she'd performed prior to her first engagement at the Persian Room.

"I was always busy. I was at the Blue Angel, the Bon Soir, and also did a good deal of television: *The Doris Day Show, The Mothers-in-Law,* and a bunch of others."

She was clearly as eager as I was to get to the subject at hand.

"The Persian Room was very different from nightclubs

Kaye Ballard traveled to her Persian Room engagements
with her toy poodle, Carmella—who was treated
as royally as any other guest at the Plaza.

today—that is, the few clubs that are still around today. The room was fabulous, and the clientele very elegant. You could tell they took time preparing to go out. Thought was put into what to wear, and the women didn't have a hair out of place. There was an air of sophistication that you just don't see nowadays.

"But I have to say, the room had the worst ventilation and circulation. Those were the days of chain smoking, and the club was cloudy. Really thick clouds. I've never seen so much smoke. Some nights it looked like I was crying, my eyes teared so much. But everything else was great."

When I asked her if anything out of the ordinary had happened to her there, her eyes lit up.

"That's easy. As part of my remuneration, I received a room in the Plaza for the time I performed, and I kept my toy poodle, Carmella, there with me."

The Plaza is and has always been pet friendly: monkeys, tigers, bears, and turtles, oh my—but that's another book.

"After my first performance, I ran to my room to check and see how my baby was. And she wasn't there! I was frantic and searched up and down the corridor on my way for help. Spying the house detective I ran to him for assistance, told him my story, and was so upset I didn't even notice he had Carmella. She was calmly walking with him on a leash. He said that someone had complained about a barking dog, and he was sent to check it out. He felt sorry for my lonely pooch so he decided to take her on his rounds with him. I was so relieved that I let Carmella go on patrol with him the entire time I was there."

I wanted to express my admiration to Kaye, as thanks for her generous spirit. "Careerwise you have really done it all," I told her. "You've been showcased on the cover of *Life* magazine, performed in shows around the world, starred in Broadway shows, and been a regular on more than one

Kaye Ballard is so beloved in her hometown of Rancho Mirage, California, that they have named a street after her.

television show. Is there anything you'd still like to accomplish?"

"I want a Tony," she admitted, "but the Tonys are all political, and I've never been good at playing politics. I'm too blunt. Ask me a question, and I'll give you my honest answer. No filter. Maybe it's because I started performing publicly at seventeen and have never stopped. Even during the early and lean years, I never had to take a job outside of show business."

Kaye's most recent project, in Santa Fe, New Mexico, is in the area of animal rescue. She and some other stars, including Liliane Montevecchi, have staged a Broadway-style show that will run into 2012, with all proceeds going toward helping her furry friends.

Driving Kaye home, I couldn't help but think that while Kaye might not have received a Tony yet, she did have a pretty impressive honor. There is a street in Rancho Mirage, California, named after her: Kaye Ballard Lane.

And, if something I mentioned earlier tickled your curiosity, you'll just have to read Kaye's book, *How I Lost 10 Pounds in 53 Years,* to get the scoop on Marlon Brando.

.　　.　　.　　.　　.

ROSLYN KIND STARTED out in show business when she was still in high school, doing demonstration records for her sister Barbra Streisand's publishing firm. After school she went to the studio and recorded songs that the company published so they had demos to send out to performers who might be interested in using them. She was fourteen when she started studying dance with Luigi Lewis in Manhattan, where she rubbed elbows with many Broadway gypsies and dancers from *Hullabaloo* and other pop-music TV shows.

"I lied about my age and didn't tell them I was still in high school," she admitted when we sat down to talk. "Two o'clock and the school bell would ring. I'd leave, get my leotard, and take dance class till—oh my God, after ten at night. Then I'd go home, get a bite to eat, and start my homework around midnight."

I'd heard that Roslyn's first engagement at the Persian Room was also her New York debut, so I asked her about it.

"Yes, my New York debut. But before that, I did a lot of other things. My television debut was on *The Ed Sullivan Show*. From there, I went on to the Hungry i in San Francisco. I also went on tour for my first album, which was released by RCA. Then I was in Puerto Rico, Oklahoma, Houston, and on and on, working on my act, all building toward the Persian Room. My act was written for me by Richard Maltby Jr. and David Shire, the guys who wrote

Ain't Misbehavin' and lots of other great shows. Some of the greatest arrangers were brought in. Lee Holdrege did my first album and Jonathan Tunick, Harold Wheeler, and David Shire were my arrangers.

"I turned nineteen while I was at the Persian Room. I remember that one critic wrote that I brought, 'a youthful essence never known to that room.' I did songs from *Hair* and *Promises, Promises* because I was young and wasn't going to do older songs. I was a little bit out of whack, with a whole different energy than they were used to. I was determined not to do stuff someone else was known for. Also, being so young, I didn't want to sing about heavy loss of love, because I hadn't experienced that. *When I Fall in Love* was actually the only love ballad I did—and it was a hopeful one—except for things that were on the charts or special material that David Shire wrote for me.

"I had a medley of 'I Dig Rock and Roll Music,' 'I Get By With a Little Help from My Friends,' and something we called the Sunday medley, consisting of 'Sunday' songs from the '40s, '50s and '60s. It included 'Sunday Kind of Love,' 'Sunday, Sunday, Sunday,' 'New York Sunday,' and others."

At that point Roslyn started singing softly, and the people around us stopped what they were doing to listen. The Beverly Hills restaurant where we sat is accustomed to welcoming celebrities and has a policy that the wait-staff is not allowed to interfere while a guest is eating. As I glanced around, I could see the servers and guests alike realizing that they were being treated to something very special, but they were all respectful and let Ros do her thing undisturbed.

"David, Richard, and I would go to the music store," she continued, "the Colony, and pick out sheet music. We spent days picking and sorting through material. I did 'Sunday Will Never Be the Same,' a hit for Spanky and Our Gang, and another hit on the charts, 'Will You Be Staying After Sunday?' They all told a story of love, and each [was] from a different decade. I didn't have any backup singers—it was just me and the Persian Room orchestra, plus my own key men: my accompanist, drummer, bass, and lead horn. Everyone else was theirs. Seventeen pieces in all.

"My act was different then from today, although I have tried to stay in the youthful bag to keep myself different from my sister. I can tell you what the ad in the paper said: 'Roslyn Kind is what you get for being good: December 17 through January 6.'

"I loved the maitre d' there, what was his name... Frank?"

I reminded her that it was John. Mr. John.

"Oh, my God, yes. He was a doll. Every night he gave me a pep talk. There was one night that Bette Davis was in the audience. Actually, I'm in one of her biographies. Someone wrote that the gentleman she was with said, 'Oh, look Bette, Roslyn Kind is here.' And she went, 'Who?' 'Barbra's sister.' 'Oh, right.'

"On that night, Mr. John told me that Miss Davis was in the room and that I should be sure to introduce her—she loved to be introduced. Well, according to her book, that wasn't exactly so. Supposedly, I put her on the spot with that introduction, but she stood up and blew kisses to everyone anyway. I'll never know the truth."

I reassured Roslyn that from what I understand, Mr. John never got it wrong. Because I wanted her to go back to some of her happier memories, I asked her whether her early shows differed from her late ones.

"Yes," she said, "and I'll tell you a story that took place when I was working out of town, getting ready for the Persian Room. One night, while I was working at a club called the CopaHavana in Oklahoma City, a big fight broke out. These drunk guys had stayed for both shows, and when they heard the same songs in my second show they got very pissed. We told them we were trying to break in a show for New York, and we had to do this material as much as possible. They were just not having it, and a big Western-style brawl broke out. I swear, people were flying over the banisters and over the bar, and my musical director signaled me to leave the stage by a different route. These guys were so rude and uncontrollable that we had to call the police.

"Afterward, I saw my manager. He had been hit in the nose and his glasses were broken. He told me not to tell his wife. I had to laugh, and I replied, 'You won't have to say a word, she's going to look at your nose and your face and she'll know!'

"That was my experience on the road, leading up to

the Persian Room, in some of the towns in Oklahoma and Texas. Thank God, in New York, you had maître d's like John to keep the weirdos at a distance."

I asked Ros whether the Persian Room had lived up to her expectations.

"My vision of the Persian Room turned out to be exactly right. I had gone there to see.... I think it was Lena Horne. So I had the gist of what it was. As I said, I was a little worried because I knew I had a younger act. But I didn't let that get in the way. I still had to be me.

"Still, God, was I nervous! But it was all very exciting. I'm not sure whether I felt more confident afterward, but maybe accepted. More like I belonged. It was an accomplishment to play the Persian Room. And it was so early in my career."

I had delicately been avoiding any discussion of Ros's megastar sister, but eventually, she brought up the subject.

"Things kind of got out of hand as I was starting my career. Originally, people weren't supposed to know who I was related to. I needed the time to develop as a performer, without the attachment and comparisons. Then I did *The Ed Sullivan Show*, and someone from my record company leaked it out. So then I had to 'evolve' in full sight of everybody.

"On top of that, the Persian Room wasn't like the little clubs, the ones in the Village where you started without the rigamarole. This was major press and major people wanting to come and see and gasp. I had to live up to a lot of

*Roslyn Kind practices for her debut
as her entourage looks on.*

things I wasn't ready to live up to. The Persian Room was
an incredibly important event for me. I felt my career was
riding on the reviews I'd get. I remember a review that said,
'Clearly this teenager's star is rising like a Saturn rocket.'"

When I asked Roslyn how she spent her days, she simply
said, "I slept late." I could only assume that meant late
nights out after her shows—but where?

"We would hang out at the hotel and have dinner. I never ate before a show—I couldn't. People would come up and visit. On opening night you would have thought my room was a funeral parlor there were so many flowers! I'm from Brooklyn, down to earth. To this day, when I'm on stage, I'm on; and when I'm off, I'm off. On stage, I'm more cocky and confident. At Carnegie Hall, I took off my shoes on stage, and that was before my sister ever did it in her concerts. Nolan Miller loaned me a pair of shoes for my gown and my toes were dying. I didn't think, 'Oh, this is Carnegie Hall, I can't do this.' And the funny thing is, people actually thought it was part of the act. I got laughs.

"Another time, sequins from my gown started falling off as I was singing. So I picked them up and asked if anyone had a bag to put them in. The audience was hysterical. I'm a very informal type of human being.

"Someone once asked me, 'what is the difference between working a small room and a major venue?' I said the trick is to make the humongous room feel like a small intimate room. That's my job. That's why I'm there, to make everyone feel that warmth personally. The Persian Room actually showed people my potential. It introduced me to the world. World-class critics for world-class papers and magazines covered me there. It was important. My sister's movie *Hello, Dolly!* was scheduled to premiere the same day as my Persian Room debut, and she made her studio move it to the next night so she and my mother could be with me on opening night."

.   .   .   .   .

SABRINA AND MARINA are settled in with me at my
favorite San Clemente beach breakfast spot, the Bagel
Shack, to visit with Jack Jones. They've promised to share
an egg bagel and sit patiently on the comfy, pillowed wicker
sofa on the outdoor patio while Jack and I visit. He's busy
putting the final touches on his new CD but has graciously
carved out some time to call in from his home in La Quinta.

I've been longing for an opportunity to talk to Jack
Jones, one of the most popular vocalists of his time—and a
very busy one I might add—for over a year, but his schedule
didn't ease up until recently. It was worth the wait.

Jack, born John Allan Jones, is the only son of actress
Irene Hervey and singer-actor Allan Jones, best remembered for acting the straight man in the Marx Brothers
films *A Night at the Opera* and *A Day at the Races*, and
for his chart-topping hit song "The Donkey Serenade."

After signing a recording deal with Capitol Records
while a teenager, Jack was invited by his dad to join him
on stage for his engagement at the Thunderbird Hotel in
Las Vegas. This was Jack's first professional gig. They sang
duets, including "The Donkey Serenade," and then he sang
a solo, his first in front of such a sizable paying audience,
and he liked it.

Capitol Records and Jack soon differed on the direction his music should go, and they parted ways. He found
that the progressive record label Kapp was a much more

compatible match. The first song they recorded together, "Lollipops and Roses," snared Jack a Grammy for Best Pop Male Vocal Performance. This was swiftly followed by "Wives and Lovers," which earned him another Grammy and a spot at the table with the big boys: an engagement at the Persian Room!

Jack entertained sold-out audiences many times at the Plaza, starting with his first appearance in December 1964 and continuing through October 1975.

"That was my debut," says Jack. "I was scared to death and excited at the same time; I had hit the big time and had hardly paid any dues at all.

"John Springer was my PR guy, the top PR guy in New York, and he handled the opening, doing a marvelous job. Everyone was there. Leslie Caron was going with Warren Beatty—they were both there—and of all the people in the room, I forgot to introduce them. Warren was a friend, and he kiddingly gave me trouble over that for a while.

"Ethel Merman was there, and yes, I remembered to introduce her. She was a good friend of mine throughout the rest of her life. So many people were there; it was a real star-studded audience.

"That entire time surrounding my first successful opening at the Persian Room was so exciting. Just prior to this I was playing a tiny club called the Living Room, so it really happened quite quickly.

"There's a funny story about that initial success. Peter Leverson worked for John Springer, my PR guy, and one day

*Jack Jones greets his biggest fan—his mother, actress
Irene Hervey—after his Persian Room debut.*

we were sitting around my suite talking on the phone, doing PR stuff, and Peter called the hotel operator for something— I don't remember what—but I heard him say, 'Operator, enough, enough. I'm talking to you from Jack Jones's suite, and I want you to X-Y-Z....' When he hung up, I remember saying to him, 'Peter, it appears that my newfound fame has gone to your head!' And we both had a good laugh."

I had read John Wilson's *New York Times* review, I told Jack, and it was very complimentary!

"Thanks. *Billboard*'s was also pretty good," Jack said modestly and matter of fact.

"I remember another time there," Jack continued. " I got a call in my suite from the maître d', John, who was a real character—very European, and he knew what to do and how to handle everything. One of his tasks was to keep tabs on who was coming to the show. So this particular night he calls and very excitedly says, 'Mrs. Kennedy is coming in! It's wonderful,' he says, and I agree, it's great. So they pull out the best china the Plaza has to offer. There are amazing flower arrangements. Her table is especially beautiful, and the staff is polished right down to their last button.

"Then John starts calling me saying, 'Jack, you have to hold the show, she hasn't shown up yet.' 'Okay, I say, but let's hope it's not for too long; I don't want the other people getting mad at me.' 'No, no, no, it will be fine,' he says.

"He calls me two or three times more with updates, basically that she's not here yet! 'Okay, but I can't hold the show much longer,' and I leave my room, go downstairs, and just wait and keep a lookout from behind the swinging door [in the kitchen].

"Finally, he comes and tells me she's cancelled, saying, 'How can she do this to me? Oh me, oh my,'and so on and so on. I say, 'You—how can she do this to *you?*' Even though I never had a chance to meet her she was reported to be a big fan."

"How long was your show delayed waiting for her?" I asked.

"About forty-five minutes by this time, but I went out and made some kind of excuse and began the show. It was fine. These things happen—you hope they don't, but they do, and you just roll with them.

"During one of the early years at the Persian Room, I was doing a show and a woman was sitting ringside with her back to me. After a while it started to drive me nuts. I kept trying to get around and look at her but she never looked, and she kept shifting to keep her back turned. Today I would have understood immediately what was what, but I didn't get it then.

"Now I'm really frustrated, but I say to myself, okay, just get through the show, get off the stage, and start looking forward to the late show. I ended the show, went upstairs, relaxed a bit, came back down, heard the introduction and applause, and thought great, this show will be fun.

"I went out, and the same lady was still there. She liked

it so much she stayed for the second show—still with her back to me. I finally figured out she was probably blind and enjoyed the music more when she was positioned a certain way."

I wouldn't have figured that out even today, I said.

I know I've asked this of other stars, but I'm curious so I ask Jack, "What did you do during the day to keep yourself busy?"

"Kapp Records was my label, and they weren't too far from the hotel, so I'd go down there and get on the phone with the DJs, which was something wonderful at that time in the record business, communicating with the people who were playing your records. Now it's iTunes and satellite radio, which is also good, but it was different then. Now I host an hour on satellite playing my records, Sinatra's records, me singing Sinatra...that's what radio is now. You don't have one hot DJ."

Jack is very much the gentleman and has made a practice of not discussing his wives and girlfriends. "It's not germane to the story," he explains. I applaud and agree with him, but I have to share one little tidbit because, after all, he told it to me—and it's cute.

"Did your wife or girlfriend—depending on the year—attend any of your Persian Room shows?" I asked.

"I think my ex-wife Jill St. John might have been there at some point when I played that room... wait a minute... she was. I remember this because we used to go around the corner to the jewelry store Van Cleef & Arpels!" (Just like a man to have his memory jogged by that!) "We also enjoyed the Palm Court.

"One of my appearance was videotaped, and this particular time my dad was there. I introduced him and got him up for a song with me, which was something I didn't want to do because he'd really been drinking. He was a recovering alcoholic, and he eventually mastered it well, but at that time he was slipping. We sang 'The Donkey Serenade' together, which went just fine. But later when I looked at that video, boy, you could see the apprehension on my face and in my eyes."

More than thirty-five years after his last performance at the Persian Room, Jack is still doing what he loves to do—singing to standing-room-only audiences around the globe.

During the '60s and '70s Jack was a staple on all the popular TV variety shows as well a guest star on the most widely watched TV shows of the day. One of his most recognizable songs is the catchy theme song for *Love Boat*. I wanted to ask him if that was his favorite song, but I felt guilty about pressuring him to soldier on without giving his overworked, raspy desert voice a chance to relax and return to the smooth crooning sound we all treasure. I would hate to be accused of being the reason his CD didn't wrap on time! Sabrina and Marina had scarfed down almost two full bagels, so it was definitely time to wind it up.

Other wonderful Persian Room
performers from the 1970s:

Edie Adams

The Burgundy Street Singers

Lana Cantrell

Judy Carne

Lisa Caroll

Jimmy Damon

Rodney Dangerfield

Daniel and Damon

Eddie Daniels

Rick Daniels

John Davidson

Vivienne Della Chiesa

Peter Duchin Orchestra

Billy Eckstine

Ethel Ennis

Errol Garner

Kelly Garret

Donna Harris and Margie Carr

Joey Heatherton

Florence Henderson

Ann Hilton

Marilyn Johnson
January Jones
Frankie Laine
Abbe Lane
London Lee
Diane Leslie
Barry Levitt Trio
The Luv Machine
Gisele MacKenzie
Charlie Marina
Al Martino
The Mills Brothers
Cavril Payne
John Rowles
Ran Sanz
Doc Severinsen
Sis and Gary
Dusty Springfield
Enzo Stuarti
Jack Wilkins
Roger Williams
Karen Wyman

EPILOGUE

The Persian Room staff was always ready to treat guests with tender loving care.

In 1974 the United States entered its worst recession in forty years. New York City suffered from high crime rates, financial disasters, declining city services, and the exodus of close to one million people. Even the famed Radio City Music Hall, with its spectacular Rockettes, was only a hairbreadth from closing its doors after almost fifty years.

*Partners in crime (and research assistants
on this book), Marina and Sabrina.*

Carol Lawrence theorized to me that a major contributing factor to the nightclub era's demise was the danger of New York City streets during that time. Club- and theatergoers feared for their safety; they stopped going to the kind of shows (like those at the Persian Room) that typically started at 11 p.m. Hotels and cabarets that counted on two shows per night to make a profit were reluctantly forced to limit performances and sadly, eventually closed their doors.

Tony Butala suggested another possible reason for the

downfall of great rooms such as the Persian Room. "They had a house orchestra and the musicians' union kept raising the pay scale for their guys, as well as dictating how many musicians had to be hired at a given venue. None of the clubs could afford it.

"The acts themselves also started to think twice. Why play an intimate room where they had to do two shows if they could get paid what the huge concert halls were offering for one show?"

Or maybe it was simply the end of an era.

The Plaza Hotel shuttered the Persian Room in 1975. The stars went on to work elsewhere and reinvent their careers. Today the Champagne Bar and Rose Room occupy the space. New York City is prospering these days, though we've had our ups and downs in the intervening years. Let's face it—nothing can really get us down!

Sometimes, when I'm sipping my cocktail at the Champagne Bar, among a sophisticated crowd clad in what passes for formal attire these days (crisply ironed blue jeans, open-necked shirts, a tunic over skin-tight leggings), I catch a whiff of perfume mingled with smoke and hear the giggling whispers of the spirits that once performed here, along with the warm applause of those who came to revel in the glamour. Then I catch a glimpse of a little girl peeking around a corner, her jumper and ponytails in disarray, a mischievous smirk on her jam-caked mouth. There is no stage at the Plaza today—but that doesn't mean the magic is gone.

INDEX

Page numbers in **boldface** indicate illustrations.

PHOTO CREDITS

THE
PERSIAN
ROOM
presents
MONIQUE VAN VOOREN
and all her assets
July 6 until July 25
Monday–Friday 10 P.M.
Saturday 9:15 & 12 P.M.
call PLaza 9-3000

THE PLAZA

Persian Lamb.
Matt Monro sings songs of fantasy and sh
ck in the Persian Room, November 2 until N
Monte and Burt Farber play the she
floor.

Who do
Marty Allen. E
sian Room. B
ely at the p
ersian Roo